FEAR

OF THE

OTHER

Other Abingdon Press Books by William H. Willimon

Pastor: The Theology and Practice of Ordained Ministry (Revised Edition)

The Holy Spirit (with Stanley Hauerwas)

Incarnation: The Surprising Overlap of Heaven & Earth

Resident Aliens: Life in the Christian Colony (with Stanley Hauerwas; Expanded 25th Anniversary Edition)

William H. Willimon

FEAR
OF THE
OTHER

NO FEAR IN LOVE

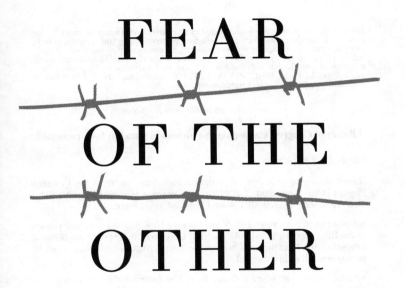

Abingdon Press

Nashville

FEAR OF THE OTHER:
NO FEAR IN LOVE
Copyright © 2016 by Abingdon Press

All rights reserved.

This book is printed on acid-free paper.

Library of Congress Cataloging-in-Publication Data has been requested.

ISBN: 978-1-5018-2475-3

Unless otherwise indicated, all scripture quotations are from the Common English Bible. Copyright © 2011 by the Common English Bible. All rights reserved. Used by permission. www.CommonEnglishBible.com.

Scripture quotations noted NRSV are from the New Revised Standard Version of the Bible, copyright 1989, Division of Christian Education of the National Council of the Churches of Christ in the United States of America. Used by permission. All rights reserved.

Scripture quotations noted KJV are from The Authorized (King James) Version. Rights in the Authorized Version in the United Kingdom are vested in the Crown. Reproduced by permission of the Crown's patentee, Cambridge University Press.

Scripture quotations marked (NIV) are taken from the Holy Bible, New International Version®, NIV®. Copyright © 1973, 1978, 1984, 2011 by Biblica, Inc.™ Used by permission of Zondervan. All rights reserved worldwide. www.zondervan.com. The "NIV" and "New International Version" are trademarks registered in the United States Patent and Trademark Office by Biblica, Inc.™

16 17 18 19 20 21 22 23 24 25—10 9 8 7 6 5 4 3 2 1

MANUFACTURED IN THE UNITED STATES OF AMERICA

To the Christians who fearlessly preached and protested against the governor and legislature of Alabama's anti-immigration law, HB 56

There is no fear in love, but perfect love drives out fear, because fear expects punishment. The person who is afraid has not been made perfect in love. We love because God first loved us. If anyone says, I love God, and hates a brother or sister, he is a liar, because the person who doesn't love a brother or sister who can be seen can't love God, who can't be seen. This commandment we have from him: Those who claim to love God ought to love their brother and sister also.
1 John 4:18-21 (CEB)

CONTENTS

INTRODUCTION

Thanks to fellow Christians Donald Trump, Ben Carson, and Ted Cruz. If not for them, I would not have been asked to write this book.

I'm serious. Competing attempts among politicians to leverage our fear of others into votes for them led to the idea of a book that thinks *as Christians* about the Other. Let the politicians do what they must to be elected by people like us, though I think they are selling us short. My job is not to worry about opinion polls, or what nine out of ten Americans can swallow without choking. My peculiar vocation is to help the church think like Christians so that we might be given the grace to act like Jesus.

A few miles from where I live, three Muslim graduate students—Deah Shaddy Barakat, Yusor Mohammad Abu-Salha, and Razan Mohammad Abu-Salha—were executed by a gunman who looks a lot like me. I am bold to believe that Jesus gives us the means to condemn, repent of, and defeat such crimes.

I confess that I have rarely been the Other. Born to relative privilege, anything I lacked at birth I made up for by youthful manipulation of American higher education and the church to my advantage, encouraged and welcomed by others all along the way. Almost nobody regarded me as a potentially threatening Other.

In conversation with a ministerial colleague, he casually recalled being a sophomore at Millsaps College. He had finally summoned the courage to ask a young woman to go with him on a date to a restaurant in town.

"Order anything you want," he told her as she examined the menu.

"It all looks so good, it's hard to decide," she said cheerfully.

They chatted about school, about this and that. And chatted.

When a waitperson finally brushed by their booth, he said, "Excuse me. No one has taken our order."

"Take a hint," she snarled and bustled away toward another table.

He sighed and shut the menu saying, "I'm not really all that hungry after all." And they left.

Did I mention that my colleague is African American?

Listening to his story I thought, *nothing like this has ever happened to me.* I can count on the fingers of one hand the rare moments when someone has reacted negatively to me or judged me unfairly because of my race, religion, gender, accent, parents, or appearance.

I have treated another person not in the way of Jesus, as my neighbor, but as the fearful, threatening Other. Though I have sometimes tried to excuse my sin as "just the way I was brought up" or due to my psychological insecurities, my behavior was in clear rebellion against the expectations of Christ.

Yet I also write as one who, solely by the grace of God, is being redeemed of my own sinful inclination to xenophobia. I have personally experienced the joy of receiving another not as enemy but as potential friend *and* the grace of being received warmly by the Other.

As bishop, I saw churches transformed in their obedience to Christ's command to welcome the stranger and in baptism, to name the stranger as family. More than one congregation, in showing hospitality to the Other, has had Jesus slip in their once closed door.

Tom Long repeatedly relates the story about his boyhood Presbyterian church in Georgia when a man in shabby clothes ambled into their church during the service one Sunday. Perhaps he was a drifter passing through, or maybe he had jumped off a boxcar on the nearby tracks, up to no good, planning to prey on people while their guard was down at church.

All they knew for sure was that he wasn't one of them.

The ushers stepped aside as the stranger entered. He was handed a worship bulletin, but not graciously. He sat by himself in a pew toward the rear. Throughout the service, pastor and worshippers cast nervous glances in his direction, wondering how he might disrupt their worship. When the offering plates were passed, folks suspected that the stranger might take something out of the plate, rather than put something in. After listening to the sermon, the man arose and quietly departed.

Though Tom was a child at the time, he recalled that after service the Georgia farmers stood under the big oak in the churchyard, talking in serious, muted tones.

"They probably didn't know how to say it," says Tom, "but everyone knew that God had put our church to a test. And we had flunked."

Tom frequently retells this story because he knows that it is at the heart of what it means to be best friends of Christ and, at the same time, his most disappointing betrayers.

In presenting our church with sisters and brothers whom we fear as the Other, God is not only testing us but giving us a gracious opportunity to recover the adventure of discipleship. By the grace of God and the ministrations of the church, we are enabled to have better lives than if Christ had left us to our own devices.

In seminary Greek class, our first attempt to translate from Greek to English was 1 John. I still remember reading the verse that sets the agenda for this book, 1 John 4:18: *perfect love casts out fear*. I recall the professor saying, "In 1 John, the Greek is easy to read, but its message is hard to live."

And how.

Chapter 1

SAVED BY THE OTHER

I was invited to a large Saturday evening youth conference where the featured speaker was Duffy Robbins, a national leader in youth ministry. Duffy opened the gathering by reading from Romans 5:6-11:

> While we were still weak, at the right moment, Christ died for ungodly people. It isn't often that someone will die for a righteous person, though maybe someone might dare to die for a good person. But God shows his love for us, because while we were still sinners Christ died for us.... If we were reconciled to God through the death of his Son while we were still enemies, now that we have been reconciled, how much more certain is it that we will be saved by his life... through our Lord Jesus Christ, the one through whom we now have a restored relationship with God. (CEB)

"I need your help with a little skit," Duffy told the packed auditorium. "As I call your name, come up and place yourself on stage. On my right is GOOD. All the way over to the left is BAD. Place yourself where you belong. First, Mother Teresa."

Duffy pointed to a young woman on the second row. "Come on up, Mother Teresa, and place yourself on this continuum of good and evil." The teenager stepped up and positioned herself well to the right behind Duffy.

"Next, Attila the Hun!" Duffy pointed to a kid midway back. Accompanied by a few laughs, Attila took his place far to the left of Mother Teresa.

"OK. Martin Luther King Jr." A teenager voluntarily strode forward and stood to the right beside Teresa. So did the next two: "Mahatma Gandhi," and "Clara Barton."

When "Joseph Stalin" and "Adolf Hitler" were called, they were welcomed on the far left by "Attila." "Barack Obama," "Hillary Clinton," "Britney Spears," and "Justin Timberlake" found their places somewhat to the left of the really, really good "Teresa" and "King."

Finally, with about a dozen teenagers positioned along the spectrum of GOOD and BAD, Duffy said, "And now I'll call up Jesus Christ." Someone giggled. Duffy pointed to a young woman who sheepishly walked up on stage. She was graciously received by "King," "Teresa," and the others to the right.

"Does that look about right to you?" Duffy asked. The crowd gave their assent. Then Duffy said, "Did you guys not listen to anything I read? I'll read it again. This time, pay attention!"

> At the right moment, Christ died for ungodly people. It isn't often that someone will die for a righteous person, though maybe someone might dare to die for a good person. But God shows his love for us, because while we were still sinners Christ died for us. (Rom 5:6-8 CEB)

"Jesus Christ" gradually moved toward the left until, by the time Duffy finished reading, Jesus was hanging out with "Stalin," "Attila," and the worst of the BAD.

"Now," said Duffy, "who here tonight wants to walk into your school on Monday morning behind Jesus?" As the band played an edgy, rock hymn, the youth streamed forward, eager to be part of Jesus's outrageous advance toward the ungodly.

Any Christian move toward the Other is based upon Jesus Christ's move toward us: "We were reconciled to God through the death of his Son while we were still enemies" (Rom 5:10 CEB).

Enemies, but for the Grace of God

When a fellow bishop was removed because of adultery, I said, "There but for the grace of God go I." Jesus taught me to say this. Fleming Rutledge tells me this phrase, "There but for the grace of God go I," was first used in the sixteenth century by John Bradford upon seeing a group of men led to the gallows. If God practiced justice rather than graciousness, if God loved high moral standards more than God loves us, we all should be headed for the gallows. Or, as Paul put it, "All have sinned and fall short of God's glory" (Rom 3:23 CEB). Not "most"—all.

"But all are treated as righteous freely by his grace because of a ransom that was paid by Christ Jesus" (Rom 3:24 CEB). Jesus Christ saves sinners, only sinners. Paul's sweeping declaration of our sin and Christ's redemption is a basis for Christlike response to the Other: "While we were still weak, at the right moment, Christ died for ungodly people" (Rom 5:6 CEB). Or, as 1 Peter puts it, "Christ himself suffered on account of sins, once for all, the righteous one on behalf of the unrighteous" (3:18 CEB).

"Joe would do anything for his family. He was a great husband and father," a speaker intoned at a funeral. Goodness toward one's family is morally noteworthy? As Eddie Murphy complained of folk who brag about how much they love their families, "That's your job!"

Of course I love my wife, my children; they look like me. When I have loved the Other, as Christ has loved me in my otherness and enmity, then that's a specifically Christian, countercultural, virtually miraculous love.

When a presidential candidate talks of closing our borders to members of one faith, speaking about them as insidious, dangerous, and threatening evildoers, I remember a TV program some years ago (during one of our many wars to end all wars in the Middle East). A group of Afghan boys had their homes and town destroyed by American bombs. Now without parents, they had fled to a safer but more wretched life in Karachi, Pakistan. They lived in a garbage dump, surviving off rotting food and living in filth.

The boys' only hope was to be received by one of Pakistan's many *madrasas*, Muslim religious schools that were infamous breeding grounds for jihadists. The boys told the reporter that they hoped to be selected as students because there they would be protected, fed, and clothed.

When asked what they thought of Americans, the boys responded that Americans were cruel killers who bomb a whole country into oblivion and ought to be paid back for their cruelty.

We have met the enemies of Christ—*us.*

I remember when Aleksandr Solzhenitsyn, a victim of Soviet repression and punishment, was invited to the United States. We celebrated our welcome of this hero of the Cold War (a deliciously in-your-face gesture to the Soviets). Then Solzhenitsyn gave a stunning speech in which he failed to condemn the Soviets but instead criticized American capitalism, superficiality, and godlessness! Solzhenitsyn really believed what he wrote in *The Gulag Archipelago*: "The line separating good and evil passes not through states, nor between classes, nor between political parties...but right through every human heart" (Aleksandr Solzhenitsyn, *The Gulag Archipelago: 1918–56* [Paris: Éditions du Seuil, 1973]).

More than one presidential candidate has recently bragged, "I will never apologize for America." Christians, on the basis of the great grace we have received from Christ, are always apologizing, confessing, and repenting. "While we were still weak, at the right moment, Christ died for ungodly people [us]" (Rom 5:6 CEB).

In the light of Paul's testimony in Romans, an important function of Christian preaching and church life is to render *me* into the Other. I am the enemy of God. I am the one who by my lifestyle and choices make myself a stranger to my sisters and brothers. I'm free to admit that because, in spite of my hostility to God, Jesus Christ has received me as friend.

I am also the one who has received grace and revelation from the Other. Even as Christ came to me before I came to Christ,

I have been the beneficiary of ministry from the Other before I was able to receive the Other as Christ had received me.

I grew up in the segregated South; I'm a product of an unashamedly racist culture. Every day I boarded a Greenville bus with a sign: SOUTH CAROLINA LAW. WHITE PATRONS SIT FROM THE FRONT. COLORED PATRONS SIT FROM THE REAR.

Nobody I knew questioned that sign, especially no one who sat next to me in church each Sunday.

My Damascus Road conversion came when my church sent me to a youth conference at Lake Junaluska and I was assigned a room with another sixteen-year-old from Greenville. When I walked in, there he sat on the bed opposite me, better prepared for me than I was for him. We had never met, even though he went to a school four blocks from mine and played on ballfields where we never ventured. He was black.

I recall nothing from the conference worship or lectures, but I'll never forget our conversation that lasted until dawn. He told me what it was like to go to his church and not mine, his school rather than mine, his world in which I was a stranger. In a paraphrase of Langston Hughes, his Greenville was never Greenville to me. By sunrise, I had my world skillfully cracked open, exposed, and also infinitely expanded and ministered to by the Other who was kind enough to help me go where I avoided.

Later, when I read Richard Niebuhr define *conversion* as "a new way of seeing," I knew he was talking about me. I once was blind, but now I see.

Commanded to Welcome

Xenophobic, exclusionary fear of the Other is more than a matter of preference for people whom we enjoy hanging out with, or those with whom we feel most comfortable. In deep fear of the Other, we separate ourselves from others in order to better oppress, exploit, expulse, confine, hurt, or deny justice and access to others whom we have judged to be so Other as to be beyond the bounds of having any bond between us or any claim upon us.

A subtext of recent debates over whether or not to admit Syrian refugees has been, "If we let them in, what's the cost? Will our nation be less secure? Will property values in my neighborhood be diminished? Will these newcomers help or hinder the economy?"

While these are not unreasonable questions, Christians ought to admit that in debates about others *Christianity's default position is hospitality, even as we received hospitality on the cross of Christ.* Sure, we can argue about how we ought to be hospitable and what steps to take to integrate these newcomers and enable them to thrive in North American cultures. We can be honest about the challenges involved in their coming to and being received as strangers in a strange land. However, as Christians, we are "prejudiced" toward hospitality, particularly for those in need, because that's the way God in Christ has treated us and commanded us to treat others.

Christians believe that the one universal God is known in a particular way in the one who lived briefly, died violently, and rose unexpectedly—Jesus Christ. God has refused to be obscure.

In this one who was fully human (like us) and fully God (unlike us), we believe that we have seen as much of God as we ever hope to see in this world.

God's move toward us enemies went against just about everything we thought we knew about God. It still does. God? God is righteous, holy, high and lifted up, glorious and good. We are not. God is up there; we are down here. Can't say anything for sure about God because God is aloof, obscure, obtuse.

And then came Jesus, challenging and refuting by his words and his deeds just about everything we thought we knew for sure about God. He was Emmanuel, God With Us, but not the God we wanted to meet. Where we expected judgment and exclusion, he enacted mercy and embrace. Where we craved unconditional affirmation of our righteousness and insider status, he slammed us with judgment upon our presumption and a call to even higher righteousness. He practiced unconstrained hospitality, inviting to his table people whom nobody thought could be saved, people whom nobody wanted saved. Resisting the clutches of the powerful and the proud, he condescended, touching the untouchable and lifting up the lowly. In his suffering, loving outreach to us, in his truthful preaching, and in his resourceful, relentless drawing us unto himself, Jesus was other than the God we expected.

This is the christological basis for Paul's command to the church in Rome: "So welcome each other, in the same way that Christ also welcomed you, for God's glory" (Rom 15:7 CEB).

The cross of Christ mysteriously, wondrously unites Jews and Gentiles, without regard to ethnicity, gender, race, or class

(1 Cor 12:13). God refused to stay singular, a monad. God is inherently self-giving, connective, and communicative. Not merely our otherness toward God but our downright enmity has been "put to death" and peace made "through the cross" (Eph 2:16 NRSV). The power of the cross was so great over the imagination of Christians that Paul could say, "I have been crucified with Christ and I no longer live, but Christ lives in me. And the life that I now live in my body, I live by faith, indeed, by the faithfulness of God's Son, who loved me and gave himself for me" (Gal 2:20 CEB).

We Wesleyans believe this is not some heroic stance reserved for a super saint like Paul; it is a presently available life based upon not only what Jesus did for us on the cross but also what Jesus daily does in us by the power of the Holy Spirit. God is not simply love but love in action, love making a way for us to overcome evil with good and to miraculously unite with others despite our various separations.

The great liberator Frederick Douglass made a speech in the tense days before the Civil War. The equally courageous Sojourner Truth was in the audience. Douglass spoke honestly and eloquently of the plight of African Americans in this country where they were held as slaves. Douglass thundered that there was no hope that white America would ever grant freedom. Whites only understood violence.

"Frederick," Sojourner Truth called out, "is God dead?"

The self without Christ is tossed to and fro, constantly under threat, the self that must use everything and everyone in ceaseless acts of self-aggrandizement and self-defense. The self with Christ is recentered, given a new identity, and rests secure in God. "It is Christ who lives in me," says Paul. That doesn't mean obliteration of our old selves but rather creates our new selves as God has created us to be, our selves with a new basis other than our old selves.

That God has enabled us to know God not as threatening, vague, distant Other but as a vulnerable, intimate friend is at the heart of the good news about God. The cross is not only revelation but also vocation. God continues to take great risk (Phil 2) in reaching out to us, refusing to save the world without us. Jesus Christ is not only God helping us but also God's incredible vulnerability in summoning us to help God's work of reconciliation (2 Cor 5:18).

First John speaks about "love" in much the same way that love is presented in Paul: *love arises not from some benign human disposition but rather as a miraculous act of God in us, in spite of us.* Love begins not with us but with Christ, the one who embodies, in word and deed, that "love is from God." Human love for each other is dependent upon the God who "first loved us."

> Dear friends, let's love each other, because love is from God, and everyone who loves is born from God and knows God. The person who doesn't love does not know God, because God is love. This is how the love of God is revealed to us: God has sent his only Son into the world so that we can live through him. This is love: it is not that we loved God but that he loved us and sent his Son as the sacrifice that deals with our sins. Dear friends, if God loved us this way, we also ought to love each other. No one has ever seen God. If we love each other, God remains in us and his love is made perfect in us....

There is no fear in love, but perfect love drives out fear, because fear expects punishment. The person who is afraid has not been made perfect in love. We love because God first loved us. If anyone says, I love God, and hates a brother or sister, he is a liar, because the person who doesn't love a brother or sister who can be seen can't love God, who can't be seen. This commandment we have from him: Those who claim to love God ought to love their brother and sister also. (1 John 4:7-12, 18-21 CEB)

Human love is symbiotic, derivative of the sort of God we've got. Christian love is responsive: "We love because God first loved us" (1 John 4:19 CEB). The indicative "God is love" leads to an imperative: (You ought to) "love each other."

This sermon from 1 John was probably voiced in a church that was facing threats from within and without, which makes all the more impressive that believers are urged not, "Be on guard!" or "Defend yourselves!" but rather, *Love!*

In 1 John 4:18, fear here seems to be specifically fear of God's judgment. A Christian need not fear God's judgments if we try to act among one another as God has acted toward us. Love, in obedience to Jesus's example, gives us "confidence" (4:17 CEB) or "boldness" (4:17 NRSV).

In loving we are surprised to have the Other move from being a stranger or enemy to the status of sister or brother. In attempting to love the Other, we find ourselves drawn closer to the God of love; we become as we profess. Love of neighbor validates that we are loving the true and living God rather some godlet of our own concoction.

The first Bible verse I memorized was John 3:16: "For God so loved me, the church, and folk who look like me that God gave..." No. "For God so loved *the world*..." It all belongs to God. No one is foreign to this expansive embrace. There may be people who are strangers to me; they are not strangers to God. There may be those who are enemies of me or my country; they are not enemies of God.

The gospel compels us to situate the Other in the story in which we have, by the grace of God, been situated. To be sure, human groups, including religious communities, share an inclination toward corporate self-aggrandizement at the expense of those outside our group. We bolster our identity and group dignity by seeing the best in ourselves and by ignoring the good in others, focusing upon the ways that others are not like us.

First John challenges us to see others differently, not denying our differences but opening ourselves to what is good, asking what God might have to teach us through each other. In other words, we are hereby urged to look at others as God in Christ has looked upon us.

Sometimes, when Christians talk about the Other, they refer to creation—we are joined together in the same human race. I find it more helpful to stress redemption—we are all the dearly loved beneficiaries of salvation in Jesus Christ.

Fleming Rutledge speaks of the relationship between loving and seeing: In 2005, Julius Earl Ruffin was released from a Virginia prison after twenty-one years of incarceration for a crime he didn't commit. An all-white jury convicted him of assaulting a white woman solely on basis of her identification of him as her assailant. Ruffin was released after DNA testing.

Ruffin's accuser, Ann Meng, did an amazing thing. She wrote to him expressing her deep regret for misidentifying him and then she testified on his behalf at the hearing to compensate him for his wrongful imprisonment. Meng said, "I feel a personal responsibility for Mr. Ruffin's incarceration. However, our system of criminal justice also must bear some responsibility. There was no one on this jury who saw themselves or their son, or their brother, when they looked at Mr. Ruffin" (Tim McGlone, "State Urged to Pay for 21 Lost Years," *Norfolk Virginia-Pilot*, February 4, 2004).

One of the great gifts of the Christian faith is not only to be able to see another as dearly loved in Christ but also to see yourself as the Other who is a dangerous threat to both God and neighbor. That's a goal of Christian preaching—to render *me* as Other. Otherwise, our attempts at gracious reception of the Other can be merely the presumptuous, patronizing condescension of those with power relinquishing a bit of our privilege to the powerless Other. It is far too easy for those who are privileged (like me!) to flatter ourselves by graciously showing a little inclusiveness toward those who have less power than ourselves. It is also tempting to rework our image of the Other so that the one who was once regarded by us as the Other is rendered into an innocuous, lovable image of ourselves.

In my first church (a forlorn, forgotten little congregation in an impoverished Georgia county), I worked for greater racial justice in our community. The lay leader of my congregation (the only person in the congregation with a high school degree) worked on an assembly line in Atlanta.

One night the lay leader called me, grief stricken. The promotion that he had been promised for a decade had been given to another.

"Did your boss give you a reason for this injustice?" I asked.

"They say it's because the company has got to promote more blacks. The man they gave the job to has worked on the line for just a few years. I'm better qualified. Preacher, when you talk about loving ever-body, I'm going to listen real hard. I'll try, but I ain't promisin' nothin'."

I was angry that the company had given him that line about their bogus affirmative action. However, I said, to my champion-of-racial-justice self, *I've never lost a job or have been passed over for a promotion by a person of another race. This man's determined attempt to act like a Christian is more impressive than mine.*

I've therefore been troubled by some of the talk about "racial reconciliation" in my own church—usually meaning the white majority being reconciled to the black minority. With the disparities of power, the centuries of white privilege, and our very different histories, an appeal for "reconciliation" implies a power equity that doesn't exist. True reconciliation is not a matter of the powerful majority giving a bit of its power to the powerless in order to burnish our positive self-image.

Have you noticed? Your being reconciled to me always sounds more agreeable than for me to do what is necessary to be reconciled to you. I'm all for reconciliation until you mention the need for reparation. Jesus lifted love out of any slough of sentimentality with, "You have heard that it was said, *You must love your neighbor* and hate your enemy. But I say to you, love your enemies and pray for those who harass you" (Matt 5:43-44 CEB). I heard renowned scholar of world religions, Huston Smith, say that Jesus's brash command to love the enemy was the distinctive difference in Christianity, a command unknown in any other great religion.

Christians believe that in the incarnation, God—considered by many to be our enemy—took on our humanity, moved in with us as the Word made flesh, loved, forgave, and called God's enemies (us!) to be God's friends, *and* commanded us to go out an welcome our enemies as God in Christ has welcomed us.

In enacting *and* commanding enemy love, we are at the very heart of the faith engendered by Jesus. It would have been breathtaking enough if God had forgiven us. Even more mind-blowing, Christ commanded us to forgive as if to say, "Though painful and costly, I have forgiven my enemies. Now you try it."

At the end of a very busy Thursday afternoon, I was cha-grinned to be encountered on my way from the church office by a shuffling, forlorn older man. Of course he was down on his luck. Homeless. "Could you help me get some food?" he asked.

Food my foot. I'm sure you will use the twenty dollars that I'll give you (just to get rid of you) to buy booze. I gave him the twenty-dollar bill.

"I guess you expect me to thank you," he said on his way down the sidewalk with my money. I told him a thank-you would be nice.

"Well, I ain't," he muttered. "Jesus made you help me. You'd have never done it on your own."

How does that man know so much about you? I asked Jesus. To which Jesus replied, *How does he know so much about* you?

My theological mentor Karl Barth in his bombshell commentary *Epistle to the Romans* famously spoke of God as "Wholly Other," *gans andere.* There is, in Søren Kierkegaard's words, an "infinite qualitative distinction" between us and God, a great gulf between Creator and creature.

Usually, the stress has been on the "Wholly"—God isn't at all like us. I wonder if it would be more biblical, and more true to the experience of lots of Christians, to put the stress on "Other" rather than "Wholly." God is not whom we expected. We thought we knew what is indicated by "God," then Jesus showed up as "the way, the truth, and the life" the only way to the Father (John 14:6 CEB), and we had to rearrange our ideas about God once we got a good look at who God really is—a Jew on a cross, arms outstretched in love of people who don't love him.

As Catholic theologian Hans Urs von Balthasar said, our salvation, as shown in scripture, is always a drama of divine recklessness and human caution, divine outreach and human refusal.

"Do you know what, for me, is the great proof of our Lord's divinity?" a professor asked as we walked out of the divinity school and onto the main quad. It was an odd question, particularly in that context. We had walked into the annual bacchanalian "Oktoberfest." Though it was early afternoon, the students had already begun drinking and carousing.

"It is that passage where it is said of Jesus, 'He looked upon the multitudes and had compassion.' I look upon this pagan riotousness and want to thrash them with a stick!" He was kidding, of course, but his remark had serious intent, pointing to the distance between our way of looking at others and that of Jesus.

When we speak of "God," we are not merely projecting our grandest notions and deepest desires and calling that imaginary configuration "God." When we say "God," we are not indicating some being who resembles us and our values, only much, much nicer. God is "Other." When we are talking about and attempting to listen to God, we are not simply expressing some of our personal notions about deity. We are in conversation with one who is Other; a stranger is in dialogue with us, interacting with us, revealing to us without lessening the sheer otherness.

When we speak to God, we are not in monologue, not just talking to an idealized projection of ourselves. We are in dialogue, not only speaking but listening, addressed by an interlocutor who expects response. Were there no difference, there would be no dialogue. We are unable to address ourselves. Conversation is demanding—we must listen and not put words into the mouth of the Other, label, or pigeonhole what we think another is saying. Conversation is risky—we may be transformed in the dialogue, hear things that we could have never said to ourselves. We become receivers whereas most of us would rather be givers; giving allows us to keep control.

Trinitarianism also says that the triune God—Father, Son, and Holy Spirit—are unified and in complete communion.

Father, Son, and Holy Spirit are distinct "persons," each having integrity and identity. These three are one.

The Father is God, the Son is God, the Holy Spirit is God; there is only one God. There is a carving on the pulpit at Duke Chapel that says, in Latin, "The Father is/is not the Son, the Son is/is not the Father, the Son and Father are/are not the Holy Spirit."

One of the challenges of Christian belief is fully affirming God's communion with us but also allowing God to be Other, to praise God as the Trinity we could not have come up with ourselves, the God who is so much more than a projection of our spiritual yearnings, a God who can command us to do outrageous things we would never have asked of ourselves, to let God be free to be God For Us without God being us. Welcoming the stranger is just the sort of communion we ought to expect from a God whose nature is relation.

Before we are told that "love casts out fear" in 1 John, we are commanded repeatedly not to fear Jesus. Isn't that odd? Angel Gabriel's word to Mary in the annunciation was "Don't be afraid" (Luke 1:30 CEB). "Joseph son of David, don't be afraid" (Matt 1:20 CEB). The angels tell the shepherds not to fear. When Jesus appears before his terrified disciples on the sea, he says, "It's me. Don't be afraid" (Matt 14:27 CEB). The risen Christ says to his disciples, "Don't be afraid. Go and tell my brothers that I am going into Galilee. They will see me there" (Matt 28:10 CEB).

Maybe it's good to be reminded that there was a time when folks feared Jesus more than the Other.

I know a church that spends three times more money on security (uniformed guards on Sunday morning, CCTV, alarms) than it spends on evangelism, welcome, and outreach. Judging from the median age of the congregation, this church will close in less than ten years.

It is the nature of the body of Christ that locked doors are ultimately more costly to the survival of the church than open doors. There is a high price to be paid for fearing the threat of the Other more than we fear disappointing Jesus.

Discussion Questions

1. The authors states that "an important function of Christian preaching and church life is to render *me* into the Other. I am the enemy of God." Describe a time in your life where you were apart or alienated from God. How is this otherness evident to you? How is God's otherness apparent to you?

2. At the heart of this book is 1 John 4:18, which includes the phrase, "fear expects punishment" (CEB). The author observes, "In deep fear of the Other we separate ourselves from others in order to better oppress, exploit, expulse, confine, hurt, or deny justice and access to others whom we have judged to be so Other as to be beyond the bounds of having any bond between us or any claim upon us." Think of examples in your life, church, community, or nation of how fear expects punishment.

3. For most Christians, "God is righteous, holy, high and lifted up, glorious and good. We are not." Is this an appropriate way to think of God's relationship to human beings? What alternative ways of thinking are supported in scripture?

4. What kind of security does your church adopt for self-preservation and protection? What message do your security policies send to others outside your community? How do you balance self-preservation with unconditional welcome?

Chapter 2

THE OTHER, MY ENEMY

A parable in the Hindu Vedas tells of a man entering a darkened room. To his horror he sees what looks like a snake coiled in a corner. Though full of terror at the prospect of a venomous snake ready to strike, he fights the urge to flee and instead moves toward the snake to examine it. Upon a closer look the specter is discovered to be nothing but a harmless coil of rope.

This, according to the Vedas, is the purpose of philosophizing—to disarm the fearsomeness of the world by removing the threat of the unknown. Knowledge of the truth about the world renders the world less fearful and more bearable.

Is there anything more natural, innate, and universal than our fear of the Other? This natural, innate, adaptively beneficial propensity to stick with our own tribe makes all the more remarkable that early on in Israel's history, God's people are explicitly commanded to "love [the immigrant] as yourself": "When immigrants live in your land with you, you must not cheat them. Any immigrant who lives with you must be treated as if they were one of your citizens. You must love them as yourself, because you were immigrants in the land of Egypt; I am the LORD your God" (Lev 19:33-34 CEB). It is unnatural enough to be told to "love your neighbor as yourself" (Matt 22:39 NRSV), but to love even the foreign *alien* (NRSV) is counter to the way we come into this world.

To be sure, there is some tension in the biblical story between God's commands not to "oppress the immigrant" and the command to exclude and drive out strangers like the Canaanites (many early American preachers labeled Native Americans as "Canaanites" and sought biblical justification for the European conquest of North America). Still, Leviticus's command not just to receive or tolerate but to *love* the stranger is remarkable.

The stranger plays a curious role in scripture, Old Testament and New. Judas, the betrayer of Jesus, threw the thirty pieces of silver on the floor of the temple and then hanged himself. Matthew says that the priests who had paid him refused to use the "blood money" for God's business. They bought a field "as a place to bury foreigners" (Greek: *xenoi*, foreigners, immigrants, strangers), casting the body of Judas among the immigrants and foreigners as if Judas was not really one of the Twelve (see Matt 27:3-10).

In Jesus's parable of the Great Judgment, when all the nations would be judged and separated, the enthroned Human One says to the blessed sheep, "I was a stranger (*xenos*) and you welcomed me" (Matt 25:35 CEB). Surprise. In welcoming *xenoi*, they had received the Human One unawares.

Ephesians joyfully proclaims to new Christians that they "are no longer strangers and aliens. Rather, you are fellow citizens with God's people, and you belong to God's household" (Eph 2:19 CEB). *Xenophobia*, the fear of the Other, stems from the Greek word for strangers.

The Neurobiology of Xenophobia

Xenophobia is not only historical; it's biological. Neuroscientists can demonstrate how our brains constantly judge whether the events or persons whom we encounter will hurt or help us on the basis of whether they *minimize danger* or *maximize reward*. When we encounter a stranger, the amygdale center of our more primitive and powerful brain functions has, for millions of years, enabled us quickly to decide whether that person is a possible reward or a potential threat, inducing in us the desire to move either "toward" or "away." Encounters with strangers require more brain work than meetings with friends, where our brains tell us to expend less energy and hunker down in our comfort zones among the familiar and the accustomed.

The neurological response to danger comes upon us faster, is more intense, lasts longer, and is more difficult to displace than the response to reward. In competition with other emotions, even strong ones like lust, fear tends to best them all in intensity of engagement of our whole limbic (emotional) system.

Science writer David Rock (*Your Brain at Work* [New York: HarperCollins, 2009]) says that our limbic system is aroused by a set of "hot buttons" that trigger visceral, intense danger response. Thanks to millions of years of evolution and social conditioning, our brains tell us to ease in toward potentially rewarding Others and to run away from perceived dangerous Others.

Rock cites research that shows when we experience a threat we (1) think less clearly, (2) have difficulty receiving and assimilating new information, (3) make mistakes in perception and interpretation, coming to false deductions, and (4) tend to respond negatively to situations, focusing on the downside and taking fewer risks.

I heard a paid spokesperson for the National Rifle Association (NRA) say that he opposed any change in America's gun laws because widespread gun ownership is the only thing protecting us from the Islamic terrorists who hate us and are attempting to kill us.

If that's true, Americans ought to ask for a refund on the billions we spend on the armed services. Is there any instance in the past hundred years of any American schoolteacher or accountant with a personal handgun protecting anybody from a terrorist? The man's advocacy for a gun in every home is a testimonial not to the facts of the matter but to the NRA's leveraging of our fears. Or should we excuse the NRA's nonsensical positions as limbic systems gone wild?

The adrenaline that is pumped into our nervous system to help protect us from a perceived threat makes us feel more confident in our judgments when in fact our ability to make good decisions is considerably reduced by fear. Our responses to external threat are more knee-jerk defensive and less thoughtful. Anxiety forces us into emergency mode, totally focused upon ourselves and our survival.

Evolution hardwired our brains to be cautious and self-protective, which made sense in a time when our survival was threatened daily. When we heard a rustle in the bushes, our limbic system enabled us to move quickly into high alert mode.

Today, these once valuable coping mechanisms are the source of some of our most damaging mistakes of judgment, including our sloppy thinking about, irrational fear of, and false consciousness of the Other.

Thousands of years safely huddling in our tribe hardwired us to regard strangers as foes until proven otherwise. In today's interconnected, interdependent world, friend-or-foe fear can be a great burden.

Clear thinking and accurate judgment are needed in order to distinguish a frightened, innocent, suffering Syrian refugee from a hate-filled, murderous Syrian jihadist. And yet our fear drives us to make unsubstantiated generalizations like, "All Syrians are..." thus foolishly lumping all Syrians together and failing to make proper distinctions.

Christians in Iraq today pay a heavy price for our ham-fisted efforts to force a new Iraq. American inability to distinguish one Iraqi from another, failing to note the deep religious, ethnic, and historical differences between Iraqis, leads to costly mistakes.

When we are fearful of another, the hormone cortisol floods the limbic system, consuming brain function as the limbic system tells our brains that we have no more important task at the moment than to focus upon the threat and fully engage our "away" response.

The neurobiology of fear may account for disconnects between the intensity of our fear and the reality of the threat. Scott Bader-Saye, in his fine book *Following Jesus in a Culture of Fear* (Grand Rapids, MI: Brazos, 2007), notes that the top killers in the United States are heart disease, cancer, and stroke. Yet our top fears are terrorists, pedophiles, plane crashes, mad cow disease, and bird flu. Though crime rates are dropping, two-thirds of us think they are rising. The population most fearful of victimization by violence (people my age) is least likely to be victimized by violent crime (young adult men are most vulnerable). A major justification for the purchase of a firearm is self-defense against bad people; most handgun deaths are gun accidents by a friend or family member, a domestic dispute, or suicide by our own hand.

Avid TV viewers are more likely than others to believe their neighborhoods are unsafe, assume that crime rates are rising, and overestimate their odds of becoming a victim, and they are more likely to own guns.

To oppose gay unions as a "threat to the family" seems to me an irrational phobia. As a pastor, I've never had a family destroyed by a gay union. Heterosexual adultery is the greatest enemy of marriage.

There seems to be a correlation between heightened fear and greater affluence. (When we lived in a Methodist parsonage, we felt little need for security guards and alarm systems.)

Our problem is not that we fear; it's that our fear is often misplaced and that we sometimes fear excessively. Too much fear is the problem as we allow our lives to be dominated by the avoidance of evil rather than the pursuit of the good.

Bader-Saye calls the manipulation and feeding of our fears the "fear for profit syndrome." Politicians, advertisers, and sometimes even religious leaders use fear as a powerful motivator, a means to exploit others for their advantage.

Training Our Fears

Though powerful and involuntary, our fears can, to a certain extent, be subject to our conscious control. Rock cites studies that show that noting and labeling our fear can reduce limbic system fear arousal.

A friend suffered from a fear of flying (aviophobia). He signed up for an aviophobia therapy group. The therapist began the first session by saying, "That you have risked signing up for this group says that you are already about 80 percent cured. Remember when you were a kid and feared going down into the dark basement of your house? How did you overcome that fear? Mother took you by the hand, led you downstairs, and showed you there was no good reason to be afraid. That's what I'll do in these sessions."

By mindful attempts to coax our brains to think through our fears, we can achieve a greater sense of overall well-being. The sense that we have choices in regard to our fear is a powerful antidote to fear. If we attempt to reframe the threatening Other in positive ways, our limbic system shifts to a more "toward" response. Reappraisal, the act of pulling the Other toward you rather than pushing the Other away, creates a neurochemical change that helps us think more clearly and act more confidently.

After hearing the NRA's Wayne LaPierre spewing forth words of hate against the president, the attorney general, and anyone who dares to cross him, my anger was burning white hot. Then I took the trouble to read some of LaPierre's speeches and, despite my revulsion, my heart went out to this sad man. Even though he is paid a million dollars a year, Wayne LaPierre must be the most frightened man in America. Fear exacts a heavy toll in the lives it masters.

Neuroscientists are learning the power of "expectation" over our brain functioning. Rock defines expectation as the feeling induced by the prospect of a possible reward, that visceral sense that something or someone good is heading our way. Expectation is thus a primal motivator of our "toward" response.

On the other hand, negative expectations tend to magnify the actual threat of others—as the data on racial profiling by police shows. If we think someone is likely to be a criminal, we tend to treat that person as a crook.

Human, All Too Human

If neurological research shows that our visceral, bodily reactions to fear of the Other have biological, physiological bases, then ought we regard fear of the Other as simply "human, all too human"? Why fight a tendency that's fixed into our bodies and brains by millions of years of development?

I bet you are ahead of me. Christianity has ample experience in condemning, resisting, and overcoming a host of perfectly natural, developmentally appropriate, innate human inclinations. The church's response to our universally shared, inherently human tendencies—such as wanting to have sex with a wide array of partners, envying others and wanting to want to steal what they have, lying, and fornicating with abandon—was to name the exercise of these predispositions as *sin*.

The church joyfully announces that God has not left us to our biological, genetic heritage, that God gives us what we need to lead more interesting and faithful lives than we would have had we not met Christ. The Wesleyan tradition has majored in the claim that though we are born in bondage to a host of masters—fear, lust, greed, pride, just to mention a few—Christ working in us has the power to produce saints. Wesleyan "grace" is the power of God that enables you to be a faithful disciple of Jesus, to be different than you would have been had you not been compelled by the love of Christ (2 Cor 5:14). Just for this chapter, define that much touted Wesleyan sanctification as the power of God enabling you to be better than your genes.

I hear objections. Christians are urged to be "realistic":

"Jesus did not mean for us to love, merely to be more just."
"This is the way it always has been and will be."
"It's either them or us."

"The evil that has been done to us requires swift, strong
retribution without pity."

"Carpet-bomb them to oblivion."

"The only way to stop a bad person with a gun is a good
person with a gun."

"They forced us to do it, it's all they understand, they asked
for it."

"It's in my genes."

"Such has it ever been, such it will always be, world without
end, Amen."

Most of these objections imply that Christians are unrealistic and idealistic. But who defines reality? Christians believe that the name for reality, all the way down, is *Jesus Christ*. We believe that forgiveness is not an impossible ideal that can sometimes be performed if no great wrong has been committed, or that forgiveness is a useful technique for bringing out the best in others—forgiveness is built into the grain of the universe by the One who has forgiven us.

It would be nice to lower our guard, to open our borders, to build more bridges than walls, but the enmity of the Other forces us into our defensive actions: "My family never owned slaves," says the one who justifies his actions as his self-protection against "black people's anger." "I didn't invent radical Islam," says another. Behind this is the perfectly understandable plea, "We are only human; this was our only choice."

The sin in such self-justification is to squelch Christian creativity, impugn the grace of God, and nullify the commands of Jesus. As Miroslav Volf says, for the perpetrator of evil against another to say, "I had no choice but to behave as I did" is itself a choice. "Either us or them" or "Stand your ground" is an act of the human will. We are not hapless, impotent victims tossed to and fro in an evil world. We have been given a choice, God has blessed us with agency, to each of us Jesus has said, "Follow me!" We need not be swept along by social convention. With all animals we share an innate, survival instinct of fear of the Other. Unlike any other animal, we can deliberate, decide to fight/flee, move away or toward, push aside or embrace. Just for now, let's define Christianity as the good news that, by the grace of God, *we have a choice.*

Created for Connection

We are created, orthodox Christianity claims, not only with a propensity to sin but also in the image of God. Lest we speak too negatively of our genetic, evolutionary inheritance of fear-of-foe and flight from the potentially threatening Other, we also ought to note the neurological evidence that we are hardwired for social interconnectivity as well.

When we perceive someone as a potential source of reward rather than threat, we are put at ease, made to feel safe and comfortable, free to consider carefully a variety of stimuli and to think more generously and therefore more clearly. In *The Happiness Hypothesis* (Cambridge, MA: Basic Books, 2006), Jonathan Haidt notes how the brain's release of oxytocin fuels our feelings of happiness and well-being. Blood pressure lowers; our sense of well-being rises.

Haidt says that studies of human happiness show that the single factor in happiness is a positive feeling about social connections—we feel that we are blessed by good friends, neighbors, and family members. Numerous studies have shown that a powerful transformer of our experience is *expectation*. Group A, when told by a doctor that a procedure "won't hurt a bit," reported half as much pain compared with those who were told "you will experience some pain from this." When brain scans were performed on subjects in these two groups while they were actually experiencing the procedure, among those who had less expectation of pain, those brain regions that normally respond to pain showed remarkably reduced activation. Expectation alters neurochemical brain activity. Positive expectations contribute to the brain's sense of joy in a way that is as powerful as a dose of morphine. Our expectation of the Other affects our experience of the Other.

Unexpected rewards release more pleasure-producing dopamine than expected ones. However, when we expect a positive response but actually receive less than we expected, our dopamine level falls, leaving us disappointed and sometimes even angry. Dopamine is a key driver and enhancer of our "toward" state, enabling us to feel more positively about others and to experience greater joy in our lives. Our desire to live happy, fulfilled lives is, to a marked degree, a matter of the right level of dopamine.

While the threat functions of the brain are strong and resilient, the human desire to move "toward," rather than move "away," can be cultivated and enhanced. Rock actually claims that we "use one set of brain circuits for thinking about people who you believe are like you . . . and a different set for those whom you view as different" (162). When we positively connect with others as friends, the pleasurable chemical oxytocin is released. Rock calls oxytocin the "neurochemistry of safe connectivity," that stimulant to brain regions that enable us to overcome our innate fear of proximity and to facilitate our approach to others. Shaking hands, swapping names, or discussing something in common actually increases oxytocin in the system. Studies of human happiness, particularly studies of successful aging, show that the key element is social connectedness.

Social disconnectedness, fear of and flight from the Other, may not be the brain's desired state. Rock cites one neurological study of women in which their brains displayed great joy in being with friends, even greater than the joy elicited by being with parents or children. On the other hand, when another is perceived as a threat, or even a competitor, less oxytocin is released.

Fear is part of our protective mechanism. Many great human achievements were initiated as a response to fear. And yet, as we have noted, sometimes our fears hinder us from the full exercise of our humanity. When is my fear of the Other inflated out of proportion? Here are some questions I might ask myself better to check my fear and to exercise my God-given choices in regard to fear:

Discussion Questions

1. Is the one you fear fast approaching or encroaching? Or is this one remote to you, making slim your chances of being harmed by this one?

2. Is the one you fear really as powerful as you fear or is this one relatively powerless to do you harm?

3. Is this one truly a threat to you or are you simply fearful because this one is different from you?

4. Is your fear of the Other causing you to turn inward upon yourself or to avoid doing things that you should do or would like to do?

5. Is your fear due to another's attempt to manipulate you and your fear to their personal advantage?

Above all, Christians ought ask the following:

1. How is God leading me, and what does God expect of me in my relationship with this Other?

2. How might Christ—the strange God we did not expect, the God who welcomed me, the stranger—be attempting to make the Other my neighbor whom I am to love as myself?

Chapter 3

LEARNING TO FEAR LIKE CHRISTIANS

'T was grace that taught my heart to fear, and grace my fears relieved," we sing in our most beloved hymn, "Amazing Grace." Grace is the unmerited love of God in Jesus Christ, the power of God working in us to give us lives we could not have had on our own. How can John Newton say that grace (1) teaches us to fear, as well as (2) relieves our fears?

What comes naturally is fear of the Other. It's one of the ways our brains protect us. What's *not* natural is to view the Other as sister or brother. Think of *church as schooling in how to manage our fears*, how to fear our fears getting the best of us, fearing the right things in the right way.

Aristotle defines insanity as foolishly having no fear.

"Aren't you afraid of cancer?" I asked a college friend as he sucked on a cigarette.

"Nope," he replied. "I refuse to live my life jerked around by fear of a bunch of stupid statistics."

He died—not of cancer; his death was a statistic of emphysema.

Courage is not the absence of fear but rather having a reason for doing the right thing in spite of our fear—fearing, revering, and honoring something more than safety. Scott Bader-Saye reminds us that fear is not always the opposite of love. Sometimes fear is validation of love. I fear for the well-being of my children because I don't want the dangers of life to cause them pain. I fear high blood pressure because it is a killer and crippler, and I like living.

Fear accompanies vulnerability. As I advance in years, I sense slightly more anxiety while driving at night, which I take to be my brain's recognition that I have some diminished physical and mental capacity. At my age I have near daily reminders that my days are numbered. While that's not a particularly pleasant insight, Psalm 90 says that "number[ing] our days" is a way to go in the gate of wisdom (v. 12 CEB). Good fear can be the result of an appropriate assessment of our situation.

Wrong fear tends to be a function of our imagination more than the reality of our true situation, fear out of proportion to the threat of the object of our fear, fear that plays upon our insecurities and builds artificial barriers between us, fear that cheats us of all that God intends us to be. While it's not wrong to fear, fear can lead us to do terrible wrong. What we need is some way to honestly acknowledge having fear without fear having us. At its best, the church teaches us to be afraid of our propensity to fear, to not fear the wrong things in the wrong way, and to fear the right things in the right way.

Fear of the Lord Trumps Fear of the Other

"Wisdom begins with fear of the LORD" (Prov 1:7 CEB; cf. 14:27) is a challenging, even offensive statement for many modern people. Ellen Davis (*Getting Involved with God: Rediscovering the Old Testament* [Cambridge, MA: Cowley, 2001], 13) suggests translating this biblical "fear" as "reverence," or perhaps "awe." (Still, where is there reverence or awe, is that not a bit scary?) The book of Hebrews says of Christian worship that "it's scary to fall into the hands of the living God" (10:31 CEB). When is the last time you were scared stiff by Sunday worship?

"Fear not" is an expression found in well over three hundred places in scripture. Jesus frequently says "fear not," but on one occasion Jesus urges fear upon his disciples: "Don't be afraid of those who kill the body but can't kill the soul. Instead, be afraid of the one who can destroy both body and soul in hell" (Matt 10:28 CEB). When I take requests for prayer on Sunday mornings, it's always petitions for healing of bodily ills, never for help with the sad state of our souls. Today we're more likely to fear for the plight of our bodies than our souls.

In light of Jesus's statement in Matthew 10:28, I'd say that when scripture urges us to "fear God," I think it means that we ought to fear displeasing God more than we fear the censure of others.

Isn't it curious that fear is the predominant Easter emotion? Why did the first to be encountered by a risen crucified Christ feel fear rather than joy? My theory is that the resurrection wasn't just a matter of a person being brought back from the dead. Rather, the resurrection was "*Jesus* is back!" That news caused consternation in those who knew Jesus best.

Jesus is resurrected, the same Jesus who commanded us to not only love neighbors but also enemies, to bless those who harass us, to welcome strangers, who has defeated death and sin, triumphed, and come back to *us*.

Scary.

Matthew ends his Gospel with the risen Christ commanding his disciples to go into *all* the world, baptizing everyone, and teaching everything he commanded—including the part about welcoming the stranger (Matt 28:19). Then Jesus promises (or threatens?), "I am with you always just to make sure you do what I order you to do" (my paraphrase).

Scary.

One evening, in high school, one of my good friends courageously refused an offer by a fellow student to engage in some illegal behavior. Afterward, when I praised him for his courage, my buddy explained, "I'm more afraid of disappointing my mother than I'm afraid of getting smacked by that jerk." So the key to courage is not the banishment of all fear but fear of the right things in the right way.

We tell our children "don't talk to strangers." Jesus demands that we welcome the stranger (Matt 25:31-46). Many of us come to church for comfort, safety, and peace; Jesus demands renunciation of security with his "Follow me!" and tells us that he brings not peace but a sword (see Matt 10:34). The major reason why most of us join a particular congregation is that the folks there are "friendly" or "just like family"—in others words, just like us. Jesus's last, great commission was, in effect, "Don't hunker down with your Jewish buddies here in Jerusalem. Get out of here. Go make disciples from *all*!" (Matt 28:19).

Our problem, in regard to fear, is that we fear the Other more than we fear the God who commands, "Love each other."

We live in a capitalist, liberal democracy organized around pursuit of self-interest, the sort of culture that values self-defense more than mutuality. The Enlightenment told us that we were all human beings, after all, born equal, with everyone deserving to be treated like everyone else.

We are discovering that the promise of Enlightenment virtues—such as equality, universal humanity, and the sovereign individual—are a thin foundation on which to build real community. A livable society is better than a gated community, a "live and let live" standoff in which everything is solved through self-assertion of claims and the aggressive gaining of power to assert one's individual rights. We live in a world of genuine inequalities of birth, power, resources, and privilege. We cannot have community without recognition of the reality of deeply different history and experience that must be honored if another is to be understood in all of his or her delightful, God-given difference. The white person who claims to be "color-blind" is often the one who tells African Americans, in effect, to "forget history." We're all Americans, after all, so lay aside your grievances and blend in with us.

The day after the murders at Mother Emmanuel church in Charleston, South Carolina, the governor (yes, the one who nine months earlier defended flying the Confederate flag over the statehouse) proclaimed, "Now, let the healing begin."

Not so fast. There can be no healing without honest confrontation and efforts to make restoration of the wounds. No reconciliation to our sameness without honesty about our difference.

During our immigration battle with the legislature of Alabama, an African-American activist told me, "Anti-immigration is not slavery. The brown-skinned Mexican has a better chance of being welcomed as an 'American' than the black man who has been here for generations. Race still rules America." That statement made the involvement of predominately African-American congregations in the fight for immigration reform all the more remarkable. A major reason why the African Americans advocated welcome of Spanish-speaking sisters and brothers into the state that had failed fully to welcome them was not their desire to adhere to the best of humanist, progressive American values but rather to be obedient to the Savior who had welcomed them.

Another ploy is to redefine the Other, or to ignore certain aspects of otherness in the Other so that the Other loses otherness. This is the old, "You're Jewish, I'm Christian, but after all, we both believe in God." This implies that our differences, even our cherished religious convictions and peculiar histories, are inconsequential. The uniqueness of your Jewishness or my

Christianity melts if we agree that being a Jew or a Christian is less important than being a modern, thinking, sensitive human being.

At an allegedly "interfaith dialogue" event, the leader began by announcing that Christians, Jews, and Muslims were united as "Abrahamic faiths," giving us more or less the same scripture and common history. By his skillful, liberal redefinition of us, we were now capable of fully understanding each other if we would just relinquish some of our differences and affirm one another as "Abrahamic."

A Christian responded, "I never heard much about Abraham at my church."

The rabbi said, "If your grandmother didn't die in a concentration camp, it will be very hard for you to understand Jews."

The imam quipped, "If we are all so much alike and have so much in common, what's there to discuss? Let's declare victory and go home."

When immigrants are received into the United States, they must show that they are the victims rather than the perpetrators of injustice. This seems to me like sensible immigration policy. But let's be clear: God doesn't require Christians to make distinctions between the "guilty" and the "innocent" in our reception of the stranger. In commanding us to love our enemies and to pray for those who persecute us (Matt 5:44), Jesus doesn't say that our enemies are not really our enemies or our persecutors' persecution of us is only apparent. Nowhere does Jesus urge us to forgive others because their sins against us are inconsequential.

We are commanded only to act toward others as God has acted toward us.

Did I say *only*?

Victims of injustice want that injustice named and condemned. Good. Judgments can be made against evil done by another, but Christians make those judgments with confession of the possibility of our own complicity in the sinful acts that we condemn, with differentiation between the perpetrator as a person (that is, a dearly loved child of God), and his or her wrong actions that are an offense against God and neighbor. We are to love, yes. But we are also to desire the truth, particularly the truth about ourselves and the Other. We not only dare to *tell* the truth about the Other but also to *hear* the truth from another. Above all we look upon the Other's possible wrongdoing with appropriate modesty that shows our determination not to divide the world between "us" and "them" when it comes to participation in evil. Again Paul reminds us, "*All* have sinned..."

The world is right to judge Christians on the basis of whether or not our lives show the strength of our convictions. After Jerry Falwell Jr. bragged during convocation about his concealed handgun and urged all the students at his college to arm themselves, I was enraged with embarrassment that the head of an allegedly Christian school would so distort the Christian faith.

A fellow preacher was more charitable: "Now I know how Muslim brothers and sisters must feel when they hear their beloved Islam reconfigured by hate-filled jihadists."

Jesus doesn't require that we see ourselves as "bad" and the Other as "good," attempting to transform the Other into an innocent, perfectly benign victim in order to be received by us. We simply try to see the Other as loved and cherished by God in the Other's mix of righteousness and sin, good and evil, *as are we*, embraced by the outstretched hands of Christ on the cross. As Paul says, no one, even victims, are "good," and no one is free from the need of God's gracious salvation (Rom 3:9, 20). Christ doesn't call us to love the certifiably innocent; he orders us to love the enemy.

Sentimentality is inadequate motivation for love of the Other. Mushy appeals for "love," the fallback position on these matters in much of my church, lies about the Other and ourselves, attempting to render the Other as worthy of our love or ourselves as lovable in our love for the Other. "Love your neighbor as yourself" cannot mean love your neighbor as if your neighbor were you. Only an appropriately grateful fear of the Lord is sufficient to overcome the often deep divide between "people like us" and the mysterious, sometimes threatening, "them."

Love your neighbor—yep, your poor black, rich white, Jewish, Muslim, NRA-conservative Republican, class-hating Democrat, atheist, homophobic, exuberantly lesbian—neighbor as yourself.

Let's be honest that our faith requires us to go toward the Other without regard for whether or not the Other steps toward us. The outcome of my step toward is not predetermined. Sometimes my gesture will be unreturned. I may discover that the Other is so angry at the hurt received from me and my kind that the Other will be unable to step toward me. Jesus does not promise that by moving toward the Other we will bring out the best in the Other. He commands us to act toward the Other as Jesus has acted toward us.

In the light of Jesus, simply receiving the Other is not the full justice we owe. Jesus pushes us beyond the conventional invite and welcome toward nothing short of *love*. But asking God to give us the grace to receive the Other is an essential first step on that journey. I find it helpful to be clear: I take the step toward and open my arms, not primarily because of my enlightened redefinition of the Other but rather *because of Jesus's redefinition of me.*

Created for Communion

What if God has created us not only with a biological fear of the Other but also with a will to embrace? God is shown, in Christ, to be pure will toward embrace. Maybe when we reach out and connect with the Other, we are moving toward the life God intended us to live. Augustine famously said of God, "You have made us for yourself, and our heart is restless until it rests in you" (*Confessions*, trans. Henry Chadwick [Oxford: Oxford University Press, 1991], 1:3). We are created for communion; therefore even in our isolation caused by our fear, we yearn for embrace.

What I have learned from Jesus is that we are not here by chance, left to fend for ourselves, a war of all against all, them or us, powerless in the face of my evil or theirs, victim of either my history or biology. God has created us to live with God and created us for communion with each other. I answer to a true story: In Christ, God entered human history and on the cross reconciled us to God and met all the conditions required for communion (soteriology). In the meantime, God has graciously chosen not to work alone. God enlists us to tell and show the world what God has done and shall do (ethics). God's work with us and with God's world is not done. There is relentlessness and steadfast determination in God's love for all creation. Human suffering and injustice are not the last word. God will ultimately expose the truth of every wrong and shall accomplish the reconciliation that we, on our own, cannot (eschatology). We are destined for communion.

It's hard to know which is worse: our active hatred of the Other, our negative lumping and labeling of others ("lazy," "vermin," "dirty"), or our indifference to others, our utterly unchristian apathy that fails to hear the command that Christ has laid upon us, that refuses to assume any responsibility toward the Other.

Respectful dialogue is fine. Honest give-and-take encounters are good. Yet, as Miroslav Volf has shown, Jesus expects more—nothing less than embrace. Even "reconciliation" is not as strong as embrace. You can't have a one-sided embrace. In embrace the arms open, there is waiting, the arms close, and then they open again (*Exclusion and Embrace* [Nashville: Abingdon Press, 1996], 141–44). In *opening*, there is desire for a changed relation to the Other, an admission of discontent with my self-enclosed being. I send a signal to the Other of openness and unarmed vulnerability, an invitation to the Other to risk response.

Then there is *waiting*, that painful time of betwixt and between. Waiting gives freedom to the Other to respond, if response is possible on the part of the Other. *Closing* of the arms is the goal of opening the arms, a sign of reciprocity, requiring two pair of arms. The embrace must not be a tight, smothering embrace but one that allows another to stay as another, but now as another in relationship. It is OK, even desirable, for the Other to remain a mystery to us in important ways. Then there is the fourth act of *opening the arms again*. Two bodies have not become one; they have embraced and now the Other is released. Embrace is not absorption of the Other or denial of the Other's otherness. We embrace, and then we let the Other go.

People who have endured horrendous wrongs want the perpetrators of injustice stopped. They don't want the injustice they suffered to happen to others. They want, ultimately, for the oppressor not to triumph over them. We must be truthful and privilege victims' testimony and not attempt to provide justification for or denial of the injustice they have suffered. I must not deny that it may be easier for me to receive another then it is for those who have suffered at the hands of another. A fair question is, "How much does it cost you to welcome the Other?"

A woman in my church was the victim of a horribly violent act. She was assaulted in her backyard at ten in the morning. We gave her support from the church, as best we could. We connected her with a therapist who specializes in helping victims of this crime.

A month later, she appeared at my office and asked to talk. I asked how her therapy was going. "Fine," she said, "as far as it goes."

As far as it goes?

"I'm dealing with my hurt and anger but, because I'm a Christian, I know that Jesus expects more," she explained.

More?

"I am distressed that I am gripped by this irrational fear anytime I meet on the sidewalk a man who is the same race as the man who assaulted me. Fear and hate," she added.

"I'm sure those feelings are quite natural," I said.

"Do you actually believe that God is great enough to free me from my fear?" she blurted out. "Can God help me not give this victory to the criminal who tried to ruin my life? Can God help me take charge and turn this thing around?"

Yes, yes, yes, I proclaimed to her, proud of her, proud of a God whose grace enables even victims joyfully to shout, "We are more than conquerors through him that loved us!" (Rom 8:37 KJV).

Eschatological faith in the final, good judgments of God and a willingness to give vengeance to God are fruit of a right fear of God. We have our job to do, in striving for justice, in listening to and understanding the testimony of the victim, in loving the Other who is the perpetrator enough not to lie about the Other's injustice. At the same time, we must affirm that vengeance is up to God, not us (Rom 12:13). Making history turn out right is God's self-assignment, not ours.

Exactly how God avenges wrong is up to God. When the moral order has been disturbed by the violation of somebody by oppression, it can be reestablished only by the transformative judging and redeeming action of God. Faith in God's ultimate establishment of peace with justice is necessary if there is to be hope for a word of love and humility in our own judgments against the Other. The slaves looked up from their backbreaking work in the master's cotton fields, looking toward the master's church, and sang, "Everybody talking about heaven ain't going there." Slaveholder Thomas Jefferson said that when he considered that God is "righteous," he "trembled."

In a small way, we each experience a foretaste of God's ultimate victory over human evil and human separation when we take part in the Passing of the Peace in church on Sunday, obedient to the Savior who said that if there is something separating us from our sisters and brothers, then that's a good reason to set down our gifts at the altar and go make peace. Church is the creation of a de facto world, world as God intends, as God is even yet creating the world to be. By God we are always on the way to communion.

Every time we miraculously move from exclusion to embrace, it's a little earthly experience of what one day we shall do forever. Truth and love don't stand in opposition, and a hermeneutics of hospitality doesn't relieve you from making correct judgments. In fact, our hospitality can be an attempt accurately to construe and to understand the Other. Christians ought to be better at building bridges than erecting walls against those we have injured as well as to those who have injured us.

So then, if anyone is in Christ, that person is part of the new creation. The old things have gone away, and look, new things have arrived!

All of these new things are from God, who reconciled us to himself through Christ and who gave us the ministry of reconciliation. In other words, God was reconciling the world to himself through Christ, by not counting people's sins against them. He has trusted us with this message of reconciliation.

So we are ambassadors who represent Christ. God is negotiating with you through us. We beg you as Christ's representatives, "Be reconciled to God!" (2 Cor 5:17-20 CEB)

Sadly, sometimes exclusion of the Other is presented as a Christian virtue rather than a sin. We take upon ourselves God's prerogative to judge, separate, exclude, and embrace as if it were our own. We label another as a dangerous threat and construct our mechanisms of defense. The separation of the world into "sinners" and "righteous" is a notoriously tricky business, too bound up with our denial of our sin, too caught in structures of privilege, race, and class to be done without the greatest of care and humility.

That America has the largest military defense budget of any country in the world suggests that our defensiveness is costly. That we have more people in jail than any other country in the world is a great irony—or perhaps even a great sin—in this self-proclaimed freest of all nations.

I wonder if our stress on the distinctiveness of our gender, sexual orientation, or native culture contributes to a sense of a vast, unbridgeable gap between us. They can't possibly understand us and we can't understand them. My experience is *my* experience. How dare you presume to "know just how I feel"? Are we guilty of overstress upon the uniqueness of our personal experience and our particular identity? There are lots of ways of attempting to dodge Paul's lumping of all us together as "the ungodly" upon whom God has shown mercy for *all*.

While we are so proudly asserting that "I am *me*," Christians must also stress that my signifiers like class, gender, tribe, race, and history are being reframed and reinterpreted by the infinitely more determinative qualifier—*baptized*.

God created us as having a certain amount of distinctiveness. "Male and female God created" (Gen 1:27 CEB). Yet after baptism, my gender is lived out against a primal, prior, primary claim of God's vocation of me to be more than merely male. I'm now, by the action of God, a disciple. Surely Paul isn't saying "nor is there male and female" (Gal 3:28 CEB) in the sense that baptism produces a third gender, washing off our previous maleness and femaleness. What's being washed are the culturally encoded signifiers whereby gender is used in our systems of oppression and domination. We attempt to use the signifiers to artificially build ourselves up or to put others down. Christ has made relative the world's way of naming us—even relativizing my biological inheritance. Baptism removes gender as a means of naming persons in order to discriminate against them. Both genders are empowered by the self-giving love of Christ.

Perhaps that's why I have experienced marriage as lifelong training in the reception of the Other. One reason why I think so-called "marriage equality" is a good thing is that I am indebted to marriage for constantly, all along life's way, giving me the opportunity to receive the Other who sleeps beside me, not as a matter of "sleeping with the enemy," but rather as the one who is not merely an extension of me, but nevertheless knows me better than I know myself, graciously augments the scope of my life, and calls forth the best from me. Wonder of wonders, these two very different individuals really do become "one flesh."

I wonder if that's why the church, after a rocky start with marriage (Paul, for instance, was suspicious of it), eventually embraced marriage as lifelong training in reception of the Other. If you can receive tough truth from your spouse without hating your spouse for it, then you might be prepared to receive tough truth from the one who sits beside you in the pew on Sunday, and then receive honest judgment from the one who sits across from you in the office on Monday. And if you get adept enough at welcoming the stranger who happens to be your spouse, then God sometimes blesses you with children who can often be quintessential strangers even to their own parents!

Other Faiths

One of my spiritual disciplines as a bishop was to try to spend an hour every week or so with a person who was not a Christian. As bishop, I was surrounded all day, every day with no one except well-formed lifelong Christians who had been as successful as I in manipulating the church to our advantage. It was claustrophobic.

My office was on a college campus so it was relatively easy to locate someone who was a Muslim, a Buddhist, or even an occasional Alabama atheist. After a few years of this, I frequently said things like, "I'm not sure I've learned that much about Muslims, but Muslims have taught me a great deal about Methodists." (Methodists enjoy thinking of ourselves as fairly much like everybody else if everyone were as nice as we Methodists. It's a surprise for us to learn that we are odder than we thought.)

But in these conversations I learned from the Other:

We Christians believe some really strange things that are not self-evident to everyone else. Being a Christian is not synonymous with being a thinking, compassionate American; we're weird.

There's a bunch of prejudice against Christians out there, some of it well-deserved.

Christians have made some big mistakes aligning ourselves so closely with American culture. When others look at us, they can't tell the difference between "Christian" and "American."

Jesus is so much more interesting and so much more loveable than Jesus's followers.

Like it or not, others will love Jesus and sometimes reject Jesus because of me and my lousy attempt to follow Jesus.

From these Others I also received some of the greatest compliments to my ministry:

"I realize that I had gotten the wrong idea about Christians."

"I wish God would show up to me like God has shown up to you."

"After talking with you I now believe that maybe, one day, I'll be able to forgive Christians for what they did to me."

We want those of other faiths or no faith to respect our genuine differences, as we attempt to do the same for them. In conversation we hope for encounter that may lead to embrace. In dialogue we learn better to communicate our faith and better to understand each other, to be delighted by commonalities, to make genuine contact with each other, and to marvel at our differences. Sometimes learning about another's faith differences reveals your faith's distinctiveness.

In all our encounters with other faiths or no faith, Christians ought to be clear that we are driven by an even greater desire than dialogue or better understanding. We are *commanded* to welcome, receive, even love.

The way of Jesus implies that I ought to be willing to sacrifice myself for the One who is the way, the truth, and the life but that I have absolutely no justification whatsoever for sacrificing the Other to my truth. There is no biblical or Christian justification for violence against the Other. Christ gives me no way of drawing the Other toward Christ's truth except through nonviolent persuasion, argument, demonstration, and witness.

"Father, forgive them; for they don't know what they're doing" (Luke 23:34 CEB) sums up much of Jesus's ministry, and not only on the cross. So does the resurrection. The one who, from the cross, forgives his torturers is the same one who first repeatedly, inexhaustibly forgives us. Christ's forgiveness is more than letting the wrongful Other "go his own way," Christ's forgiveness makes way for the Other, transforms the relation between the victim and perpetrators, opens up new space. The enemy is permitted to retain enmity.

These three recurring malfunctions plague contemporary Christianity:

1. exclusive identification with one ethnic, national, economic, educational, or cultural group;

2. subjective turning inward into the safe realm of personal and private as opposed to Christianity's universalistic impulse; and

3. thinking of the Christian faith as a technique for meeting individual needs and healing individual hurts rather than God's means of retaking the world.

Love in Action

A theologian of my acquaintance was recently asked about Christian love of the neighbor. She responded that talk of Christ's forgiveness and love is fine for those who have power and privilege, "but what about an African American like me who has no privilege or power to give away? I cannot believe that the command to forgive was addressed to me."

Jesus probably spoke words of forgiveness and love to victims of oppression who were chronically disenfranchised and powerless. In saying to all his followers "forgive your enemies," Jesus was not speaking about relinquishing power or acting from a position of privilege but rather seizing power in the name of the coming kingdom of God, turning the world upside down, shaking your fist in the face of those who would assume the privilege of defining your life and your world. To both the powerful and the powerless, he commanded, "Follow me!"

Jesus demanded changed hearts, obedience, and defiant acts of mercy from those who, before they met Jesus, had little power or agency of their own. Surely he spoke thus as testimony to the miraculous power of God given to those whose great need made them special objects of divine gifts. He offered not only hope but also demanded change, even among the victims. By commanding them to take charge of their lives in this way, he transformed victim into victor.

Christ did not deny injustice or sin but rather both truthfully named it and defeated it by dying on a cross for our injustice and our sin. He who knew not sin was made sin. He doesn't explain away sin as not really sin, or injustice as just the way the world works. He atones for sin. The cry of the innocent for justice is met. The enslavement of the powerful by their privilege and power is broken. Our sins against the threatening Other are forgiven that we might live differently. It is therefore possible to live into a new world even while we are in the rubble of the old world, standing for truth and justice even as we demonstrate forgiveness and grace.

It's not enough for Christians to prattle sweet sentimentalities that "all you need is love." There is hard, demanding work to be done against injustice. We must face facts without being paralyzed by them. People are afflicted when powerful people fear disempowerment by the Other. Racism is more than fear of the Other, but surely fear of the Other is driven in part by our racism. Sixty years after Brown v. Board of Education legally desegregated schools, African Americans are disproportionately the victims of violence from both police and their fellow

Americans. The only institutions in which they are overrepresented, rather than underrepresented, are prisons and the military. African Americans have considerably less wealth and shorter lives than whites. Numerous studies show that African Americans are victims of implicit, unconscious biases of teachers, physicians, police, and just about any white person whom they encounter.

Any Christian commanded by Christ to love must also work for alleviating or condemning those fears that lead society to put down or commit injustice against others. In Jesus's great story of the Samaritan and the wounded man in the ditch, Jesus expends the most verses in describing not that the powerful person had pity upon the victim or felt love toward him, but rather that he stopped, risked attack by the criminals who had beaten and robbed the man, put him his donkey, made arrangements for his care at the inn, and even promised to repay anything that was expended in caring for this stranger. "Go do likewise," Jesus says, "love your neighbor in need even as I have loved you."

Love of God and keeping the command to love is a way of overcoming the world (1 John 5:1-5), of rising up and taking action against the ways of the world. Christ has freed us to do what our culture finds difficult: to be bound to each other, bound even to the Other. To risk embrace, to dare to take responsibility for each other, can be the defiant act that raises the church out of our inclination to sappy sentimentality or middle-class mediocrity.

Jesus is more than an advocate of tolerance and inclusivity for whom the chief sin is lack of diversity. He came preaching not tolerance but rather God's radical, gracious inclusion of sinners at God's table. Jesus said more than, "Show hospitality to your neighbor." He commanded us to love. And as Miroslav Volf reminds us (*Exclusion and Embrace*, 73–74), Jesus preached not only love but a changed heart and life, demanding it even (maybe especially) of those who considered themselves "insiders." He reworked once stable definitions of what was "clean" and "unclean" (Mark 7:14-23; cf. 5:25-34). Jesus reached toward and transformed those possessed and ostracized by "unclean spirits" (Mark 5:1-20). He shocked his inner circle by proclaiming that excluded tax-collectors and whores were gaining entrance into God's kingdom before us presumed good ones. He condemned those of us who used our religion to build walls of false purity or to construct a barrier of false righteousness (Mark 7:15), ridiculing those who prayed, "God, I thank you that I'm not like everyone else" (Luke 18:11 CEB). He castigated our desire for purity, saying that many who pride themselves on their practice of goodness were no better than contaminated sewage (Mark 7:19). Jesus gets into all manner of trouble because of who he supped with.

If we are not sure that Christians and Muslims worship the same God, I am certain that we cannot worship God who is Jesus Christ without also being under compulsion to encounter and embrace. Love is actually movement toward the Other, doing something for brothers and sisters, not just having the right slogan or attitude. As Dietrich Bonhoeffer said, love in action is so much more significant than "love in our dreams."

A group of church women in North Carolina, during one of our wars to end all wars in the Near East, wrote letters to mothers in Iraq, expressing their dismay at their country's actions, showing concern for the suffering that Iraqi mothers and their children were going through.

"We have no idea what difference our letters make," said one, "but we're fairly sure this is what Christ expects and, if we do what we can do, he'll take our offering and he'll do the rest."

Jesus told a famous story about a divided family in which the younger brother demands an inheritance that was not rightly his and then wastes it in loose living. When he finally returns home in rags, his own brother, who stayed home, refers to him in front of their father not as the brother he is but rather as "this son of yours." The older brother then presents his prodigal sibling in the worst possible light to his father and refuses to come in and party.

And where is the Father at the end of the story? The Father is out in the darkness, pleading with the brother, who has now become the Other, to come join the celebration, to be in communion with his brother, to let God's party begin.

That's what God does and what God invites and enables us to do, too.

Discussion Questions

1. Give some examples of attempting "to redefine the Other, or to ignore certain aspects of otherness in the Other so that the Other loses otherness."

2. How is your church or workplace identified with people who are the same in race, ethnicity, economic

class, or cultural affinity? How are these markers a barrier to others?

3. The author identifies a problem with "thinking of the Christian faith as a technique for meeting individual needs and healing individual hurts." How does this thinking inhibit or contribute to God's mission for the church? How does the focus on personal needs communicate with persons who are Other, that is, different from your group?

4. Think of a person who is or was your enemy. What changed or would need to change for you to love your enemy?

Chapter 4

LOVING THE OTHER IN CHURCH

I'm opposed to churches pausing in worship and asking, "Are there any prayer requests?"

It's not that prayer, *Christian* prayer, is bad. It's just that in every church I visit, I never hear any prayer requests of any need other than for physical healing *of people in that congregation.*

There's nowhere in scripture that practice passes for prayer in Jesus's name. Jesus's peculiar approach to prayer was not to urge us to compile a list of all our sick friends and family but rather to "pray for your enemies."

How strange is the way of salvation in Jesus Christ.

The *au courant* tendency to reduce the purpose of the church and its ministry as meeting my needs, soothing my cares, healing my hurts, and fixing my ills is a distortion of the gospel. Of course the poor, the hurting, the sick and wounded, the addicted and alienated, the doubting and the lonely are subjects of special care by the church. But church is not where we get what we want out of God; *church is God's means for getting what God wants out of us.* Church is where, if we're doing our job, we meet Christ whose main work is accomplished not by healing and helping but rather *vocation.* Christ helps and heals by giving us outrageous assignments, insisting that we feel someone else's pain greater than our own, take responsibility for someone who is not in our family, welcome strangers as we have been welcomed. Thank goodness Jesus doesn't wait until we are in good health, without pain, secure, and free of fear before he commands, "Follow me!"

I was pleased when our congregation received a big offering for the victims of 9/11. However, I was much more excited when our church made an even larger contribution to victims of an earthquake in Pakistan. The victims of 9/11 resemble me and my clan. How wonderfully odd to feel a modicum of responsibility for people far away who neither look like us nor like us.

A major way that Christ saves is by thrusting us toward the Other. In moving toward the Other, the church gives us the opportunity to be gracious givers rather than self-absorbed consumers and receivers. We are freed from the human tendency to construct less demanding gods (idolatry), concocted to serve our desires and fears. Jesus gives us the means to be with the Other, not as somebody, after all, much like ourselves but rather as the one whom Christ loved, for whom he died, and whom Christ is determined to have at all costs.

When a young white criminal walked into a Bible study at Emmanuel AME Church in Charleston, South Carolina, and gunned down a group of African Americans, a little, predominately white United Methodist congregation in South Carolina immediately made plans to go to the victims' funerals in order to show their outrage and solidarity with the victims. They also became engaged with the shooter's family who lived a couple of miles from the church. If the world wants to understand why a group of people behaved this way toward the victimized Other and the perpetrator Other, the world must listen to a story about a God who behaved this way toward us.

Church as the Wide Embrace of Christ

Romans 9–11 shows Paul gripped by a sweeping vision of God's kingdom bursting beyond one chosen people to all. An inheritance that was promised to a few is now graciously bestowed by the Lord "who makes the ungodly righteous" (Rom 4:5 CEB).

Isaiah had heard a sweeping promise (Isa 40–55) of God's salvation extending beyond Israel into all the nations in a new age in which

> the wolf will live with the lamb,
> > and the leopard will lie down with the young goat;
> > the calf and the young lion will feed together,
> > and a little child will lead them.
> The cow and the bear will graze.
> > Their young will lie down together,
> > and a lion will eat straw like an ox.
> A nursing child will play over the snake's hole;
> > toddlers will reach right over the serpent's den.
> They won't harm or destroy anywhere on my holy mountain.

The earth will surely be filled with the knowledge of the
  Lord,
just as the water covers the sea. (Isa 11:6-9 CEB)

The promise sounds even more bodacious in context—Israel's tragic exile. With the heel of the Babylonians on their necks and good reason to spew words of hate against their oppressors, Isaiah poured forth poetry, affirming that one day, some way, God would have all, including even the Babylonians.

Indeed, in the prophetic witness, there is testimony to the possibility that God is great enough even to use our enemies (like the Assyrians in Jeremiah) in God's attempt to rescue God's chosen people from their forsaking of their vocation. (Martin Luther King Jr. frequently told the African-American church that it had a special call to help white Christians and their churches to be more faithful.) Believing that there is only one God encourages us in encounters with even the most hostile Other to consider the prophetic possibility that God is moving toward us in the Other. The Other may be regarded by us as Other, but is never an Other to God. The Other may be an enemy to the United States, but God is not an enemy to the Other. The Other may hate us or God, but God loves the Other.

So when Saddam Hussein infuriatingly bragged, "We Arabs will teach Bush how to be closer to God," Christians say, "God has used worse than you to instruct us." Having been told that Saddam was such a monster that we must remove him, we now face the irony that Christians are persecuted in the new Saddam-free Iraq under a government we put in power. The wars we launched to pacify the Near East fueled the morphing of the

Taliban into al-Qaeda, then into the horribly violent ISIS. If we had feared Saddam in the right way, would we be dealing with the sad, unintended aftermath of the most expensive, longest war in our nation's history?

In Romans 11, Paul's prose breaks into a hymn of praise to God's far-reaching wisdom and gracious judgments in offering us a world that is so much better than the one we have fashioned through our fears: "All things are from him and through him and for him. May the glory be to him forever" (Rom 11:36 CEB). "Do not become proud, but stand in awe" (11:20 NRSV).

We make our rigid distinctions between us and them, enemies and friends, insiders and outsiders. Then along comes God who blurs our boundaries by making "the sun rise on both the evil and on the good" and sending "rain on both the righteous and the unrighteous" (Matt 5:45 CEB). And all our neat, haughty distinctions ("I may not be the best person in the world, but at least I'm better than those murderous Muslims") are blurred by God's gracious sun and rain until we can't tell the Other from us.

We experience the love of Christ on a personal scale—compare Wesley's Aldersgate insight that "Christ died for *my* sins, even *mine*." Paul makes this personal love global. A man in my church told of descending out of the clouds for a bombing raid in Vietnam. He was aghast, as the clouds cleared, to see in his sights people emerging from a Catholic Church.

"Nobody told me Catholics were big in Vietnam. I couldn't pull the trigger. They looked like my church in Iowa."

65

Narrow parochialism is the modern nation with its vaunted claims of sovereignty and its murderous defense of its humanly constructed boundaries. A universal, expansive, inclusive notion of the human race is the Roman Catholic Church.

God's Love Even for the Gentiles

The outward, Other-oriented quality of the gospel permeates the Acts of the Apostles. Imagine that you are huddled in your house church with early Christians somewhere in Asia Minor. You are Jewish, as are your fellow Christians. Though on different paths, all of you have come to the astounding conclusion that this strange Jesus of Nazareth is indeed the long-awaited Messiah, the fulfillment of God's promises to Israel. You have concluded that events in Judea a century ago—the birth, life, crucifixion, and resurrection of Jesus—turned the world upside down: God has at last come to redeem God's people. Though you are few in number, sometimes harassed, often ridiculed, but mostly ignored by your pagan neighbors, your *ecclesia*—"the called out" or "church"—believes that it is the first wave of the onslaught of the God's long-promised realm. God's people will at last get the heel of the empire off their necks, and these Gentiles will get what's coming to them.

The risen Christ has told us that we will be witnesses to this good news (gospel), scattered from Jerusalem, the center of our faith, all the way to "Samaria, and to the ends of the earth" (Acts 1:8 CEB). It doesn't take long for that promise to be put in motion. At Pentecost, the Holy Spirit descends upon "Jews from every nation under heaven living in Jerusalem" (Acts 2:5 CEB), empowering us to speak up and to hear each other, even though we were separated since Babel by different languages. When a crowd in the street mocks the Pentecostal commotion, Peter preaches to his fellow Jews that the Spirit's regathering of Israel includes not just those in the room at Pentecost but "you, your children, and for all who are far away—as many as the Lord our God invites" (Acts 2:39 CEB). It's a divine reversal of the "scattering" that occurred at the Tower of Babel when we used our unified language to "make a name for ourselves" (Gen 11:4 NRSV) by building a great tower that would be grander than God. God scattered us, dividing us into many languages, pushing us out of safe comfort zones of monotonous speech.

At Pentecost, God brings us back together, not on the basis of imperial governmental projects and monolithic human schemes, but in terms by the Spirit. Now the scattering of languages will be used by God, not for separation but rather for missionary spreading of the good news. In God's future, everyone will be able to speak to and to understand each other in spite of our differences.

So why should we be surprised when Gentiles begin showing up? When Peter said that the promises are for "everyone who calls on the name of the Lord" (Acts 2:21 CEB), we quite naturally assumed that meant *us*, not *them*.

Acts is the story of how the church deals with the shock that "God has enabled Gentiles to change their hearts and lives so that they might have new life" (Acts 11:18 CEB). A group of Samaritans asks Philip for baptism into the Way (Acts 8:12).

Samaritans, though antagonistic, are at least distant relatives. But then Philip meets an Ethiopian in the desert and baptizes him (Acts 8:26-40), a man with whom we have nothing in common. Greater shocks were to come. In Acts 10, Peter baptizes the first Gentile convert—a *Roman army officer*, Cornelius, and his whole Gentile family!

Imagine what it must have been like to be in a congregation of fellow Jews and to see even *Gentiles* drawn to Christ as their Savior, outsiders and persecutors embraced by the One who was meant to embrace *us*.

Reception of the Other (Gentiles) was the major challenge for these early congregations. In Acts 15, the church has a meeting in which there is an argument over what to do about *them*. Must these Gentiles become Jews (i.e., for the men, circumcision) in order to be baptized? Circumcision and fidelity to the Torah had kept us Jews as Jews through centuries of diaspora and Gentile persecution. How could Christians maintain continuity with Israel and worship of the one true God if they disregarded the clear claims of scripture?

At the end of the meeting in Jerusalem, James quotes Amos (Acts 15:16-17) as justification for welcoming Gentiles and as a promise that the historic, biblically ordained wall between Gentiles and Jews would be broken down. Gentiles would be expected minimally to keep kosher and, most importantly, circumcision—the indelible marker between Jew and Gentile—would not be required for baptism.

The greatest hope for the contemporary church is that God's enlisting us to assist God's move toward the Other is deeply im-

bedded in the church's DNA. The birth of the church at Pentecost is followed by hundreds of rebirths as the church of each age
is confronted with the question that consumed the Acts 15 meeting: *Will we follow the expanding boundaries of the God's kingdom
or not?* Will we attempt to keep up with the roving, seeking,
searching Holy Spirit? Will we risk welcome of the stranger as
Christ has welcomed? Will *we* respond to *them* as Christ?

The book of Acts goes on to say that once the Holy Spirit
commandeers the church, there is no more "private property."
Sharing and communion are visible signs of resurrection (Acts
6). This early communitarianism is the vision the church dares
to keep before itself to judge present arrangements. God's open
invitation to risk becoming a human gathering is more interesting than being a Kiwanis or Rotary member. This is God's revo-
lutionary rearrangement of what is "mine."

When the church keeps boundaries permeable and porous,
we're not relaxing our standards, we are fulfilling our historic
vocation to try to be half as welcoming of others as Christ has
welcomed us.

Acts makes receipt of the Other at the heart of Christian mission. Embrace of the Other begins in the heart of Jesus Christ.
Cornelius and the Ethiopian, even the selection of Church Enemy Number One, Saul-to-Paul, to be the lead missionary to
Gentiles (Acts 9), shows that God's kingdom grows as the Holy
Spirit embraces those whom we, if left to our devices, would exclude. *Mission* is the name for when the Christian goes to, listens
to, presents the gospel to, dares to serve, and risks being changed
by the Other.

Mission denotes that Christ expects more than "invite" and "welcome," more even than "hospitality" to the Other, certainly more than humbly "being with" the Other. We are commissioned to the active, searching, seeking, embracing love of the Other.

Any congregation where there is no growth, no shocking baptisms, no tense meetings full of argument and conflict over what to do about contemporary "Gentiles" is indicative of a church that's failing to obey Jesus. Any pastor content to run errands for the faithful, to care and to comfort church members, is allowing church leadership to be degraded into keeping house rather than participating in the expansive reach of the One who said not only "I know my own sheep and they know me" (John 10:14 CEB) but also "I have other sheep that don't belong to this sheep pen. I must lead them too" (John 10:16 CEB).

When I praised Lutherans for the clarity of their preaching and the beauty of their liturgy, a Lutheran bishop said, "You Wesleyans set the bar for all of us in evangelism and outreach." If true, that makes all the more sad that in my church "evangelical" has too often become degraded into "I'm to the right politically" or "I don't want LGBT people ordained." Sad that "progressive" often means "I am to the left politically" or "I want slogans about inclusiveness and diversity but don't want to do the hard, risky work required to make my church a place that energetically receives new members of the body of Christ." The Wesleyan revival was, in great part, a movement of the Holy Spirit away from parochial, established "parish" ministry out into a "world is my parish" encounter with the Other. John Wesley dreamed of a church where those who had been excluded as too poor, too un-educated, or too addicted to gin to be within the reach of Christ were shown *salvation for all!*

In the last decades, The United Methodist Church has spent millions on programs to foster more ethnic diversity in our church, had numerous meetings on the subject, and praised our-selves for being inclusive. A 2015 study by Pew Research showed that our church has gone backward in diversity. Methodists are less racially inclusive than more than a dozen other denomina-tions. We were content with electing a more diverse Council of Bishops, staffing general church committees by quota, and hav-ing catch slogans about racial inclusiveness rather than equip-ping our pastors to lead and holding our people accountable to the work required to have racially diverse congregations. How very un-Wesleyan.

In one of my former congregations, we sought and eventu-ally welcomed as a member a woman who was, due to her ad-diction, homeless. A family was assigned to lead the church in doing what we needed to do truly to receive Alice as Christ had received us. We had two years of successes and disappointments, frustrations and wonderful surprises, hard work that stretched our patience and our finances.

When Alice had been off alcohol for a year and was thriving in a new job, I thanked the woman who was instrumental in her recovery.

"You should thank Alice," she responded. "Before she joined Trinity, we were in danger of becoming a club for sweet old folks. Alice made us a *church*!"

Welcoming Alice restored the adventure of salvation in Christ and saved us from moderate, mediocre Methodism. After Alice, we changed our evangelism slogan from "We welcome you" to "We NEED you."

Gathered to Gather

A curious dynamic of separation and welcome is at the heart of the church. The church is "called out," *ecclesia*. Why? We are gathered from a world of natural xenophobic fear of the Other for the purpose of God's gathering of an odd people who look different from the world's assemblages. Our particular service is to announce the good news that Christ has kicked down the walls we have built between us and is miraculously gathering us into "one body" with "many [members]" (1 Cor 12:13, 14 CEB). The Spirit does not erase our bodily inscribed differences but enables us to be one by loosening the superficial, humanly constructed differences imposed upon us by our social roles and our culture. Jesus says that in his Father's house are "many rooms" (John 14:2 NIV). Every time the church gathers, the diversity of those gathered testify that God's house is capacious there is room for me and room for the Other.

The church is a showcase to the world of God's determination to love and to rule the world—all of it. We are called out, made peculiar and distinctive in order to show the world a living, breathing, visible demonstration of the power of the Holy Spirit to overcome our natural, perfectly understandable human tendency to gather people like us and to exclude people like "them."

Hospitality in the name of Christ is more than a slogan about "inclusiveness" and more than a warm welcome. ("Let's not love with words or speech but with action and truth" [1 John 3:18 CEB].) Christian love is love in action, a move to incorporate, and a strategy that draws somebody into the body in such a way that we know that our church is truly Christ's church.

Making Love in Church

> Be wary of your friends!
>> Don't trust your sibling!
> . . . .
> One cheats the other;
>> no one tells the truth;
>>> they train themselves to lie;
>>> they wear themselves out by doing wrong.
> You live in a world of deceit, and in their deceit
>> they refuse to know me,
>>> declares the LORD. (Jer 9:4-6 CEB)

Not exactly "love your neighbor" sentiment. Neighbors and friends are characterized as untrustworthy slanderers, deceitful oppressors. But note: Jeremiah says these words to his own people, to Israel, the people of God—not to the enemies of God. Amazing to be in service to this sort of God!

When 1 John says there's no fear in love, "love" is within the context of the Christian congregation. Matthew's Jesus commands love of enemies. Luke's Jesus makes a despised Samaritan an example of a neighbor. But in the Johannine writing, love is churchly, intramural. When Jesus says, "I give you a new commandment: Love each other" (John 13:34 CEB), it's love in church. Some have taken this tendency of the Gospel of John to be delimiting and isolationist, a parochial confinement of Jesus's outrageous enemy-forgiving love that characterizes the other Gospels.

John thus reminds us that the most difficult love assignment by Jesus is to love the Other who sits next to us in church. I confess that I've found it easier to have positive feelings for Muslims than for some of my fellow United Methodists. It's curiously easier to love neighbors across the ocean than the annoying guy next door. At my church's General Conference, we see the sad results of those who believe that sexual differences are more important unifying qualifiers than "United Methodist."

In 1 John, Jesus calls his disciples "little children" (1 John 2:1; 2:12, etc.). I wonder if calling us "little children" is more than a term of endearment—it's an all too accurate description of church people who, though we are called to be God's children, often act like unruly, spoiled brats.

If we love Jesus, we're commanded to love fellow followers of Jesus. If we can't somehow find a way to love Jesus's friends, we'll never figure out how to love Jesus. "If anyone says, I love God, and hates a brother or sister, he is a liar, because the person who doesn't love a brother or sister who can be seen can't love God, who can't be seen" (1 John 4:20-21 CEB). Give thanks that elsewhere our Lord said, "Allow the children [i.e., the bickering, self-centered, whining brats] to come to me" (Luke 18:16 CEB)!

It is tough to love fellow Christians, especially when engaged in fierce disagreements with fellow Christians. I was present during a fierce debate over the significance of sexual orientation for the ordination of church leaders. During the debate, one of the disputants said, "This is a matter of upholding scripture."

His antagonist countered, "You are not commanded to love the Bible; you are commanded to love your Christian brothers and sisters!" He had to be thinking of the letters of John.

Jesus doesn't say that loving each other in the church means there won't be disagreements. Tertullian said that one reason why the early church grew was that the world looked at them and said, "See how they love each other." But Tertullian was often a crabby and combative antagonist with his fellow Christians. Some churches, rather than love each other, decided to have a truce with each other, so fearful were they that the church would disintegrate during disagreements.

Jesus commands us neither to agree with each other, nor just get along with each other, or tolerate each other—Christ's people must love as deeply and broadly as Christ loves us.

Church for Others

Reception of the Other can be a saving experience for Christians who thought America was "our" world where we reigned as cultural custodians. The African-American church has always known that they were "strangers in a land that belongs to others"

(Acts 7:6 CEB), a countercultural community, God's outpost. Nothing is more countercultural than our belief, engendered in us by Jesus, that our identity is secure in God—not in our nationality, race, gender or any of the other ways the world demarcates human beings.

Miroslav Volf (*A Public Faith: How the Followers of Jesus Christ Should Serve the Common Good* [Grand Rapids, MI: Brazos, 2011]) urges the church to cultivate a "hermeneutic of hospitality" in our relationship with Muslims. In contrast to the popular "hermeneutic of suspicion," where we expect something sinister beneath the surface of the Other, a hermeneutic of hospitality

1. accepts the other's self-presentation, looking for good in the Other; and

2. makes judgments, interprets, and assesses with an openness engendered by our knowledge of God's basic stance toward humanity.

We behave in unashamed human imitation of Christ whereby we were transformed from an enemy of God to a friend by God's sheer grace. We gather to worship God as relational Father, Son, and Holy Spirit who are one. We "make believe" we are hospitable, so that, by God's grace, we believe the promises of God and live what we profess. The church gives us experiences just threatening enough to enable us to experiment with new ways of living without being so threatened that we are paralyzed by fear.

Let's be honest about how the church can be a threat to hospitality. The boast of a "strong, tightly knit youth group" can signify an inwardly focused clique that allows no intrusion. Paul calls the church "the body of Christ," a joining together on the basis of what Christ does, not a "family." One can be adopted into the family, but membership is up to the family. We are in this body, not due to open-minded acceptance by its members, but rather because all have been made members by Christ.

We investigated hiring a young man to initiate a "pub ministry" for our urban congregation that is surrounded by many hip bars and coffeehouses. He told us how he would attempt to establish Bible study and prayer groups in some nearby bar or café. We got excited about the prospect of luring twenty-somethings to our aging congregation.

Then he said, "But be clear what we're up against. If I should meet someone in one of those bars and say, 'Hey, why don't you let me pick you up and we'll go to church at that big church just up the street,' that is equivalent of saying to her, 'Hey, let's sleep together at my apartment tonight.'"

What?

"I would be asking her to go against everything she holds dear. She believes this church is homophobic, old-fashioned, racist, the cause of all violence in the world, and judgmental of what she did last night. You are asking her to lay aside her fear of you and walk in your church."

It was good to be reminded of what it may cost the Other to accept our offer of Christian hospitality.

As a pastor it's easy to be consumed with running errands for those who come to church because that's safer than leading outreach to those who are not here. The "friendly church" is often a congregation that puts so much into "us" that little room is left for welcoming "them." Showing hospitality to the stranger has become an important ministry of the church that finds itself in a fearful world where hostility to the Other is commended as patriotism.

On a certain Friday, a presidential candidate made a particularly nasty remark about "Mexicans" messing up America. By that Sunday we went to church. I was hoping our pastor might make a statement about the candidate's racist comments. She didn't. Rather, after her sermon, she invited forward a family from Honduras who had been attending our church. She baptized their youngest daughter and the mother as well. She told us that God expected us to take responsibility for the care and nurture of this family and that they were expected to lead us in a new ministry to Spanish-speaking people. The church stood and affirmed our citizenship in the kingdom "which Christ has opened to people of all ages, nations, and races."

This is the way the church protests loudmouthed politicos, this is our go-to solution for putting right what's wrong with our society. *The church*.

I know a church that gratefully received a biracial family. Then another. "We have some folks who drive thirty miles to be here on a Sunday," bragged the pastor. "Those families reversed two decades of decline in our membership. Turns out, there's a bunch of people out there just dying for a church that will help them be the people they want to be, a church that shows that Jesus can do what America can't."

The governor of North Carolina, ahead by more than thirty points in the polls on the eve of his sure election, ran scurrilous TV ads showing a searchlight shining on a group of rough-looking people slithering under a fence in the darkness. Pat McCrory's voiceover promised that if elected governor, he would protect North Carolina's borders from illegal immigration (even though North Carolina has no borders with other countries!).

When I protested McCrory's anti-immigration ad, a parishioner said, "You should be more concerned that we elected him by a huge margin. Maybe if you were a better preacher, we would be better voters." Ouch.

The last book of the Bible, Revelation, says that in the end, when God gets what God wants, a great cloud of worshippers will be gathered: "After this I looked, and there was a great crowd that no one could number. They were from every nation, tribe, people, and language...[shouting], 'Victory belongs to our God!'" (Rev 7:9-10 CEB). If you want a foretaste, a glimpse of that eventual blissfully universalist crowd, attend church next Sunday.

On the way to that promised heavenly bliss, here are some practical steps your church can take to welcome and receive strangers.

1. Lay leaders must ask their clergy to discipline themselves to spend half as much time visiting, witnessing to, and getting to know people who are not (yet) members of our congregation as time spent with members.

2. At every gathering of the church, visitors ought to be expected and explicitly invited to be part of the congregation.

3. There must be active, personal strategies, not just for inviting and welcoming others but also for receiving and integrating them into the body. Christian love is more than right slogans and good ideas; it's love in action, active encounter, sustained life together.

4. Every member of the congregation should be expected to participate in face-to-face, self-sacrificial service to people in need in the community and to discover the joy of receiving good things from the people we thought we were helping.

5. Every congregation ought to do an honest inventory of all the ways that the congregation unintentionally excludes or makes it difficult for Others to be in the congregation. Locked doors, unfamiliar practices, unofficial dress code, distribution of leadership and power, music, accessibility, and lack of expectation and follow-up with visitors can all be factors that contribute to newcomers' sense that they are not welcome.

6. Are there groups or individuals in the congregation who feel voiceless or alienated? What specific steps can be taken for listening and understanding in order to be more hospitable to those whose beliefs and opinions may be counter to the predominant congregational ethos?

7. The reality of fear of the Other is a fit subject for Bible study, sermons, prayer, and honest discernment in the congregation.

8. Which specific economic, ethnic, racial, or political groups evoke fear from the majority of the congregation? What can the church do to move toward these groups and offer the church as a safe place for honest conversation, listening, and better understanding?

9. When a Christian or group of Christians makes some exclusionary or hateful statements or act against a non-Christian group in your community, make contact with the targets and let them know that these Christians do not represent the truth about Jesus Christ.

10. If there are those who have been victims of injustices perpetrated by the Other, those whose fears are stoked due to hurt by another, the church can support these victims by showing sympathy for them and by reassuring them Jesus Christ is powerful enough to help them move through their anger, hurt, and fear toward, rather than away from, the Other who has wronged them.

Receiving and Being Received by the Other

"Spirituality" is all the rage nowadays—feeling religious, sort of, without bothering with Jesus's body or having to be religious with the Other. John's frequent, boringly repetitive "love each other"—clearly meaning the person next to you at the Lord's Table—makes me think that maybe John sometime served a United Methodist church.

John commends loving each other not only as sign that we are a well-functioning congregation but also as a means of witness to the world. The words are not, "God so loved the church and people like me that God gave…" No. "God so loved *the world*" (John 3:16 CEB, emphasis mine).

Jesus told a story of a banquet in which those first invited guests make ridiculous excuses for refusing the invitation (Luke 14:16-21 NRSV). The host orders his servants to "go out at once into the streets and bring in the poor, the crippled, the blind, and the lame"—just the sort of Others with whom we never attend a party.

The story ends with the first invited (*us*), by their own actions, excluded from the banquet while those who were considered outsiders, Others (*them*), at the table.

Whether Jesus's parable is heard as good news or bad depends on where you happen to be when you get the news. For the Other, away from the table, the good news is that God is the one who invites, who is determined to throw a party for all. For those of *us* who have degraded Christ's table into a comfortable, smug, boring, homogenous gathering of people like us, in excluding the Other, we excluded our Lord.

As a bishop, I occasionally received the credentials of clergy calling it quits. Never once did I have a Methodist preacher throw in the towel because of Jesus. One would think that there would be many preachers who say, "I give up! Can't continue to work for the Word Made Flesh. Jesus is just too demanding!"

More typical is for clergy on their way out to say, "I love Jesus but can't stand his friends." They're committed to church in general, but specifically desire to choke to death the chairperson of the altar guild.

I left academia to become a bishop. Sometimes people asked, "What do you most miss about life in the university, compared with your life now as church bureaucrat?"

I answered, "I miss most the Duke Office of Admissions, which ensured that I would never work with anyone who was not like me—same background, same gifts for manipulating the system to my advantage. Church, on the other hand, is notoriously nonselective. We pastors are forced to work with anybody whom Jesus drags in the door!"

Hallelujah.

Discussion Question

The author gives ten practical suggestions for welcoming and receiving strangers. If you are reading this book in a group, you have implemented suggestion number seven. Of the ten suggestions, put a mark or highlight next to the practices that your church is implementing. Then select one or more suggestions that you will personally champion for the sake of your church and community.

Chapter 5

JESUS, THE OTHER

Tell me, what must *I* do to have eternal life?" demands the lawyer.

"Simple. Love God with everything you've got and your neighbor as yourself," replies Jesus.

"But who is my neighbor?" he persists, implying love is easy, neighbor is not. If I can figure out who is my neighbor, carefully differentiating between those who are worthy of my neighborliness and those who are not, I will love my neighbor. What is the latest trend in neighbors?

Jesus answers, as he so often does, with a story (Luke 10:25-37). A man on the road from Jerusalem to Jericho gets beaten up, left half dead in the ditch by robbers. There he lies, dying, hurting, forsaken. Down the road comes a priest. (Crowd perks up.) But the priest, rather than helping, passes by on the other side. (The crowd loves it. "Go get 'em, Jesus. We are sick and tired of these money-grabbing, self-righteous, TV preachers from Tulsa. Sock it to 'em." The mob is always anticlerical.) Then, down the road comes a Levite, a lay leader of First Church

Jerusalem. He passes by on the other side. ("Great!" says the crowd. "Those Levites who sit on front pew every Sunday and act so damn pious. They think they own the church just because they are the top ten tithers. Go get 'em, Jesus!")

There lies the man in the ditch.... You hear more footsteps coming toward you. The sun beats down. You know you've lost a lot of blood. This may be your last hope. You open your eyes, blurred by loss of blood, and you see coming toward you—a humble, sincere, religious, but not showy, ordinary Methodist person like you. No. You see...a *Samaritan*!

No, not a Samaritan! We Israelite insiders hate Samaritans— racial mixers, heretics. We would wade through the Jordan just to avoid meeting them on the same road. (In Luke 9:54, James and John want to call down fire on the Samaritans.) *A Samaritan! I'd rather die than to be saved by the likes of you!* Jesus's critics sneered, You are a Samaritan and possessed by a demon! the worst thing they could say (John 8:48).

And you know the story. The Samaritan stops, risks his life (after all, the bandits who put the man in the ditch could still be lurking in the shadows), rips up his expensive suit for bandages, dresses your bloody wounds, puts you in his Lincoln, takes you to the inn, and pays for everything, telling the innkeeper to look after you and he will foot the bill.

It's not that the priest and the Levite were bad. They are identified as full-time religionists. An important function of religion is to enable us to make distinctions between the innocent and the guilty, victim and oppressor, the deserving and the undeserving poor.

You can't help everyone in need. You don't know how the man in the ditch contributed to his plight. Above all, he's not your problem. You've got your hands full looking after family and friends. There must be limits. It's just too dangerous to stop on an interstate these days. It's illegal to pick up hitchhikers. You have no medical training.

The Samaritan's help is oddly excessive, extravagant in his goodness, in taking time, risk, and sacrifice for this perfect stranger in the ditch. Most of the verses in Jesus's parable describe in great detail the extravagant, risky nature of what the Samaritan did for a dying man with whom he had nothing in common.

We like to think of the Samaritan as a decent sort of fellow—like us. He writes a check to the United Way, donates blood to the Red Cross, or volunteers at the public school. But these are all things we can afford, gifts without risk—$25 a year, a pint of blood, an hour a week. Our giving tends to be another form of self-love, a shrewd and cautious way of making ourselves look good.

"All you spend," the Samaritan tells the innkeeper, "I will repay when I return."

Jesus asks, "Now, think clearly, Mr. Theologian, who of the three was the neighbor?"

"Wait," says the lawyer. "I asked you who is my neighbor, whom should *I* love as I love myself?"

The odd thing is that Jesus reverses the lawyer's question. Not, how can *I* be a neighbor to strangers, but *which stranger is neighbor to me?* Which of these three—the good priest, the well-known Levite, the despised Samaritan—was a neighbor to the wounded man in the ditch? Which of these three should the wounded man love as much as he loves himself? Not "to whom should I be a neighbor?" but *who is a neighbor to me?*

And the layer begrudgingly replies, "I guess, I suppose it was the one who had compassion. The Samaritan."

You must put yourself in the right place. With Saint Augustine, I doubt this is a story about a victimized man in a ditch to whom we strong ones are to be charitable; it's a story about three people who came down a road one day and only one was a neighbor—a despised Samaritan.

We'd rather die than be the recipients of this sort of neighborliness.

The lawyer who wanted to justify himself, to be sure he was on the right side in regard to love of God and neighbor, is confronted not by poor wounded man in a ditch but by the anything-but-poor Samaritan—the despised, rejected, disgusting Other. The lawyer wondered who was dependent upon him only to be cast by Jesus into a position of need and dependency upon another who must take risks, make sacrifices, and dare to minister to him. The Other is the neighbor whom the lawyer saw as enemy.

Three people passed by—a preacher, a committed layperson, and the only one who stopped was a member of ISIS, or the NRA, or the PLO. Fill in whomever you most fear and despise.

And we responded in unison: *We'd rather die than be saved by the likes of you.*

So once again we are surprised that, as in so many of Jesus's other parables, this is not first of all a story about us and what we resourceful ones must do to show a little hospitality to those less fortunate than ourselves. It's a story about the strange God we didn't expect, the God who sometimes saves us through people we can't stand. It's not a story about how we can save ourselves by doing this or that good deed but a story of the strange way Jesus saves.

We, like the lawyer, want to know the limits of our responsibilities toward others. How can we distinguish worthy recipients of our love? Who are the deserving poor? How much are we supposed to give? Who is *my* neighbor?

But the story is not about to whom are *we* are to be neighbors. It's about who is a neighbor to *us*. Who is that Other coming toward me, the scary Other whom I fear who just might save me if I were to risk embrace?

Remember, this argument with the lawyer is preceded by the charge of "this man welcomes sinners and eats with them!" (Luke 15:2 CEB). This one welcomes prodigal sons, forgives adulterous women, and admits thieves into paradise. This one claims that God's sun shines on the good and the bad. "Father, forgive them," he says even as we tortured him to death. This one then returns in resurrection to the very ones (*us*) who betrayed and forsook him. This one's love relentlessly risks reaching out, reaching down—making our charity look miserly.

The despised, offensive Samaritan Other who saves is *Christ*.

We are dying in the ditch, proud and alone. Our unexpected neighbor is the one whose love is so extravagant that it saves. Here is a story, not about the difficulty we good ones face in deciding who deserves our neighborliness but the difficulty we all have in seeing this despised stranger, this Other, Jesus, as neighbor.

The lawyer's question—*Who is my neighbor whom I ought to love as much as myself?*—is answered. It is this despised Samaritan-like savior who, though he was God, risked all, stooped down, washed feet, healed, spread out his arms toward us, and died. Our problem is not only that we don't know who are our neighbors; we don't know who is our God.

The rabbi leaves the lawyer and travels up the road toward Jerusalem. There, at the end of the road, we betray, mock, deride, strip, beat, and crucify this Samaritan. He came to the wounded, the naked and the lonely, dying. We looked upon him and said in unison, "We'd rather fearfully hunker down here with folks like us than risk welcome of those whom you embrace. We'd rather die than be saved by the likes of *you*."

In your church and mine, by the grace of God, we are being given neighbors we wouldn't have known without Jesus and a Savior who is determined to bring all things together, even us.

Hope for the Other (or for us in our fearfulness) is that Christ's risky, determined love is strong enough to defeat our fear.

Thanks be to God!

Discussion Questions

1. Think of a time when you were traveling through an unfamiliar, strange place. Describe the people or

situation that made you feel uncomfortable. Share ways to overcome this fear.

2. Read aloud the parable of the good Samaritan in Luke 10:25-37. For the people within your reach, who is the neighbor that is served the least? Which neighbor poses the most risk? Share ideas about how God can help you overcome the risk for the sake of the Other.

BIBLIOGRAPHY

Augustine. *Confessions*. Translated by Henry Chadwick. Oxford: Oxford University Press, 1991.

Bader-Saye, Scott. *Following Jesus in a Culture of Fear*. Grand Rapids, MI: Brazos, 2007.

Davis, Ellen. *Getting Involved with God: Rediscovering the Old Testament*. Cambridge, MA: Cowley, 2001.

Haidt, Jonathan. *The Happiness Hypothesis*. Cambridge, MA: Basic Books, 2006.

McGlone, Tim. "State Urged to Pay for 21 Lost Years." *Norfolk Virginia-Pilot*, February 4, 2004. Qtd. in Fleming Rutledge, "My Enemy, Myself," in *Not Ashamed of the Gospel: Sermons from Paul's Letter to the Romans*. Grand Rapids, MI: Eerdmans, 2007.

Rock, David. *Your Brain at Work*. New York: HarperCollins, 2009.

Solzhenitsyn, Aleksandr. *The Gulag Archipelago: 1918–56*. Paris: Éditions du Seuil, 1973.

Volf, Miroslav. *Exclusion and Embrace*. Nashville: Abingdon Press, 1996.

———. *Public Faith: How the Followers of Jesus Christ Should Serve the Common Good*. Grand Rapids, MI: Brazos, 2011.

SCRIPTURE INDEX
(BY CHAPTER)

4. Loving the Other in Church

5. Jesus, the Other

SCRIPTURE INDEX
(BY REFERENCE)

Scripture Index (by Reference)